Praise for *More Than Great*

Mike and Diane bring years of experience to bear in this book, from their own marriage as well as from years of ministry. This has led to this very practical as well as inspirational book that has the potential to transform your marriage. More than theory, this book gives practical steps of action for any couple, whether they are in crisis or simply needing a tune-up.

—Dr. Ronn Read
National Chaplain for Man in the Mirror

In their book, *More Than Great,* Mike and Diane Siri offer not only a lifetime of marriage experience and wisdom, but also practical tools to help any marriage. To walk through this book will lead you to not only a transformed marriage, but also a transformed life. We have already seen our marriage benefit from this and can't wait to continue to live an epic marriage!

—Rob and Laurie Bergman
Directors and Co-Founders of Simple Life Missions

More Than Great inspired Heidi and me to pursue the covenant marriage God intended—one rooted in intimacy with Him, ourselves and each other. When you go to God's Word and trust His truths, an epic marriage isn't just possible—it's promised.

—Greg Lucid
President of Lucid Creative

As the daughters of Mike and Diane, we've experienced the words in this book long before they were written.

Growing up, we didn't see the ins and outs of how our parents worked at their marriage, but what we did know was that their devotion would always be to each other first, that they had tremendous value for bettering themselves as individuals, and that they always had, and always would, rely on God to lead them. We watched them go through many seasons of life, including complete career changes, navigate times of great loss, and pursue their God-given purposes while supporting each other every step of the way. They taught us the value of true intimacy by teaching us how to know ourselves and how to be known and loved by God. That created a culture in our family of having deep and meaningful conversations that ultimately shaped all of our relationships.

As adults, we've watched them pursue God's design for marriage and have seen the fruits that have come from not settling for just a good marriage. It's an example that continues to inspire us and a legacy that will live for generations to come.

—Kate Hathway and Molly Beatty

MORE THAN GREAT

Discover God's Design for an Epic Marriage

MICHAEL AND DIANE SIRI

Published by
Orison Publishers, Inc.
PO Box 188
Grantham, PA 17027
www.OrisonPublishers.com

Contact the authors at mike@therelationshipcenter.org.

For our kids and grandkids,
that their marriages may be
more than great!

Acknowledgments

For 13 years we had the pleasure and blessing of being mentored by Pastor Harry Stackhouse, an amazing man of God. He discipled our family in all things spiritual, including sharing his heart for marriage with us as well as with our daughters and sons-in-law. We miss his gentle spirit and revelatory teaching.

More Than Great evolved from The Epic Marriage Workshop created in 2014. The material has increased in effectiveness as a result of the feedback shared by those who have experienced the workshop, as well as those who guided the book's creation, including our coach and agent, Keith Carroll, and Marsha Blessing and her team at Orison Publishers, Inc.

Our thanks go as well to all of our friends and family members who have supported and encouraged the Epic Marriage ministry and the creation of *More Than Great*.

CONTENTS

OUR STORY

WE WERE 30-PLUS YEARS INTO OUR MARRIAGE when Diane made the comment, "We're in trouble!" She wasn't saying that we were headed for divorce; rather, she was saying that we were not on the path to achieve what God created and desired for our relationship to be. She was right.

Our marriage was very good, but it fell short of what it could be. We had been deceived into believing that our marriage had reached its destination when the truth was there was much more joy available to us. Thus, our journey required an adjustment in order to move beyond "very good."

We began to pray and talk about what that meant, and we sought a new revelation of what marriage was created to be.

We were led to the realization one morning that on the traditional scale of one to ten that we so often use in rating something, the increase from one level to the next is often viewed as minimal, both in the change that is required and in the reward that is received. And although the usual descriptor for the top of the scale is "great," is it worth the effort to strive to get from a seven to an eight?

What if the impact looked more like the Richter scale, where every move up is a tenfold increase in energy? Yes, every one-point improvement in our marriage would require a consistent tenfold increase in the work required to get there—but the benefit would be tenfold as well. On this scale, we didn't consider a one-point increase to be minimal.

Plus, our new scale didn't top out at "great"; rather, the pinnacle is designated as "epic."

A level ten marriage would be beyond great—it would be *epic*!

We decided that's what we wanted. Then we made the decision to pursue it with all of our heart!

Not long after, it became apparent that our revelation was not just about our personal choice to strive for an epic marriage; we were also being led to encourage and guide other couples toward the same goal. We had witnessed an increase in broken marriages and families resulting from evil attacks intended to separate God's children from Him, and we believed it was God's desire and plan to bring revival through the restoration of marriages and families. What Satan intended for evil, God would turn for good!

Our part was twofold. The first was for me (Mike) to focus on being a mentor to husbands and fathers by simply sharing the wisdom I had gained through our marriage journey. Part two was for us to partner in working with couples on their relationships with themselves individually, with God and with each other.

Fast forward ten years…

On our 45th wedding anniversary, we watched the sun set over the water while dining at a lovely Italian restaurant. We celebrated our time together as husband and wife, and we reflected on the long list of life events we had shared—many for the better, some for the worse, but all of them *together*!

We agreed that our decision to follow God's plan for marriage has produced more joy than we ever thought possible. It has given us the desire to pursue intimacy with ourselves individually, with God and with each other, as well as the freedom and courage to work toward becoming all that we were created to be within a marriage that reflects God's perfect design.

Both of our daughters are now married and, along with our sons-in-law, are choosing to not settle for a marriage less than epic. We desire for epic marriages to be a part of our family legacy and have committed to pray and declare daily that our five grandchildren and their future spouses will also make the same commitment.

More Than Great: Discover God's Design for an Epic Marriage was born out of a dream we had. We wanted to create a way to pass on to future generations the wisdom God had given us through our journey toward an epic marriage. Today, you are holding our dream!

We are grateful that God has led us on this journey and that we are able to share it with others. Our hope and prayer are that you will also choose to strive for your marriage to be epic and that you will hear God speak those wonderful words:

"Well done, good and faithful servant....Enter into the joy of your master." (Matthew 25:21)

Mike and Diane Siri

PART 1

GOD CREATED MARRIAGE, AND IT IS PERFECT!

CHAPTER 1

WHERE ARE WE?

WHEN WAS THE LAST TIME YOU WENT to a shopping mall with your spouse?

Online shopping has drastically curtailed our mall-shopping visits these days. But in the early years of our marriage, shopping malls were opening up all around us—one of which claimed to be the largest in the world at the time. We were both a little overwhelmed on our first visit. What stores were there, and where were they located? We had no idea.

As a stereotype, when a woman enters a mall, she is often there with no destination or specific path in mind. Her "need" is to shop. But when a man enters a mall, he's most likely there on a mission, hunting for something specific. He has determined in advance that he has a "need," and he has a type of store in mind where he can fulfill that need.

If the two of us are making the trip together, we are probably on the hunt for something specific. *That's our need.* If we are unfamiliar with the mall, we will head to the nearest "Mall Directory" for guidance. First we'll find that green dot on the map with the descriptor "You Are Here." *That's our starting point.* Then we'll locate the store that will most likely accomplish our mission. *That's our destination.*

With all three pieces—our need, our starting point and our destination—identified, our path becomes clear. But our journey doesn't really begin until we *choose* to take the first step.

That holds true for growth and improvement in our marriage relationship as well. We have to determine that we have a need, know where we're at, and have a clear understanding of our destination. Then we must choose to begin the journey.

With regards to your marriage...

Where are you?

What is your need?

What is your destination?

Are you ready to take the first step?

THE STARTING POINT

Two simple questions altered the course of our marriage journey:

1. On a scale of one to ten (ten being the best), how would you rate your marriage as it exists today?
2. Are you content with your marriage—"yes" or "no"?

We both agreed that our marriage was very good—about an eight on the scale. I (Mike) answered "yes" to the second question; I was content with our marriage. I had been deceived by the world's standard into believing we had reached our destination: a very good marriage. Fortunately, Diane wasn't!

According to God's design, our marriage fell short of what He intended it to be. We agreed to pursue a new vision of what marriage was created to be and adjust our journey so that we were on the right path to get there. We have discovered in the subsequent years that there was much more joy available to us, all due to the simple decision to pursue an epic marriage.

We agreed that we had a *need*. Our "You Are Here" green dot—our *position*—was partly determined by our ranking. Determining our ranking required us to be intentional about reviewing the quality of our marriage rather than just thinking that "our marriage is our marriage; it is what it is." For us, the answer to the first question was encouraging. Then we added in the answer to the second question, and our starting point became more obvious. And our need became clearer!

When we began to use those two questions with the groups of couples we counseled, we discovered three things. The first was that spouses seldom rated their marriage the same—and were surprised by the other's answer. The second was that very few couples both rated their marriage above average. And finally, many—*too many*—were content with an average marriage.

In the process of reflecting on our own marriage, we both gained a great perspective on our view of where we were at and the realization that those views were slightly different.

Diane's Story

I do believe that since marriage is created by God, then marriage must be perfect. The two people in the marriage, however, are not perfect. Mike often credits me for starting our journey towards an epic marriage because of my statement, "We are in trouble!"

But when I look back at when and why I said those words, I see that they came from my selfish desire of wanting him to change because I was not happy. I wasn't really thinking of our marriage; it was more about what *I* wanted.

We were in a time of transition, and I didn't think Mike was as joyful as I was about doing house projects. Of course, I'm always full of ideas about what needs to be done—while Mike is the one doing them. We *were* in trouble, though, because my heart was more about getting than giving.

What I have come to understand is that the marriage relationship is about giving. Giving, however, can only be the purpose if Christ is in the center of that marriage relationship and if God's design is what we strive for.

Thankfully, Mike and I were in agreement that we needed to change the path we were on.

The reality is that our answers and reflection can be encouraging but are most often humbling. They give us our starting point and, hopefully, a desire for something better. They lead us to ask, "Should we continue on the current path, make a slight adjustment, or take a new path altogether?" If our marriage is better than average and has been steadily improving, we should continue on our current path. But if we are stuck or falling, then it's time to make a change.

Still, knowing where we're at, along with the realization that our marriage could be better, doesn't convince us to take the first step *until* we clarify our destination and conclude that it's worth the bother.

WHERE ARE WE GOING?

When we ask people the question, "What's wrong with marriage?" we hear about things that have gone wrong, such as poor communication, selfishness, lack of trust, adultery, growing apart, different goals and/or dreams, lack of passion, fallen out of love, etc. We often see confused faces when we respond back by saying, "*What if we told you there is nothing wrong with marriage?*"

If marriage is created by God, then marriage must be perfect.

First Timothy 4:4 says, "For everything created by God is good...," referring to the original form of what God created. Since one of the things God created is the marriage relationship, then in its original form, it is "good." We usually use the word *good* as a rating, but in the sense of God's creation, *good* describes something that is absent of evil. Perhaps a better translation of the Bible's original language is that God's marriage creation is *properly beautiful*. Properly beautiful! Is your marriage properly beautiful? That sounds more like *epic*, more like what a couple envisions when they say their vows during their wedding ceremony.

In subsequent chapters, we will dive into God's reasons and purpose for creating the relationship of marriage, what His design looks like, and how we live that out. For now, we just need to absorb the following description of where we are going:

Epic describes something or someone that extends "beyond the usual or ordinary."[1] If we commit to and begin a journey toward an epic marriage, we will begin to experience a level of joy that is beyond our usual or ordinary experience. At some point, our marriage will surpass that level of usual or ordinary that exists in the vast majority of marriages in the world. Then, one day, the level of joy we experience in our marriage will be beyond what we could have ever imagined. It will delight us and take us by surprise. On that day, we can celebrate that we

have achieved what God created and designed: a relationship that is properly beautiful...*epic marriage*!

Doesn't that sound like an amazing destination?

Yet, even knowing where we are at and realizing that there is an amazing destination ahead, we still have to decide to take that first step. What will inspire us to step out and start our journey?

The short answer is *wisdom*.

Both of us believe that our decision to pursue an epic marriage was because the vision for what was available didn't come from man but from the Holy Spirit. We had no way of knowing what would actually result from altering our course, but we knew by faith that there was something better.

Years later, we have the wisdom to say that the vast amount of the joy in our life is a result of both of us committing to live out God's design for marriage. Our kids, grandkids, work, home and daily life together—those areas of our life that bring us great joy—are built off of the foundation of our marriage. We are grateful for the wisdom we have gained because God revealed a different destination and journey than the one we were on.

Mike's Story

Interestingly, God continues to bring forth wisdom because of the path we have chosen, each new insight resulting in greater joy. One of those revelations came when I was sharing my journey with a friend. As I was telling him that our level eight marriage was often a nine approaching an epic ten, I felt one of those proverbial taps on my shoulder and God whispered, "Your marriage is more like a five or six."

There was no criticism or condemnation in His words, but rather a powerful realization...there is much more revelation, wisdom and joy available to us than our minds and hearts can imagine. He would bring each new insight forth as we were able to receive it, and we would continually walk in awe and wonder at His perfect design of epic marriage! We have come to know that the destination He created is amazing, but we also realize it is a journey that is to be lived out and celebrated each day.

As counselors, we often deal with people who are conflicted because they are not applying what they know. Their conflict is between their knowledge and their behavior, which means they lack wisdom.

But the wisdom we are referring to is not just the application of knowledge we have gained through the insight of life circumstances. Rather, it is the practical application of *revelation knowledge—* knowledge that is revealed by God through His Holy Spirit and that convicts us to change by accepting God's design!

We often have the opportunity to share the joy and benefit we have experienced through our marriage with an individual or couple seeking counseling. Some are not ready to begin their journey toward epic marriage. They lack the wisdom to see what is available due to life's distractions (such as kids, finances, woundedness or fear of change). Our hope for them is that they will pause for a moment to receive the revelation God is trying to give them.

Many times, only one of the spouses has gained wisdom and is not content because his or her marriage relationship is not heading toward the proper destination. Our hope and prayer for them is that they will continue to seek counsel individually as well as have the strength and patience to wait for their spouse to receive the revelation knowledge that God is trying to bring forth.

Some couples who seek counsel from us have already received that revelation knowledge, and they are like sponges as they seek understanding of what their journey could and should look like. There is great joy for us when we mentor these couples.

Yet, in all cases, what we share with individuals and couples is *wisdom* when it comes out of our mouths, but only *knowledge* when it hits their ears. They still need God to change their knowledge into wisdom.

Experiencing an epic marriage relationship is *simple* (just live out God's design for marriage), but it is *not easy* to achieve. It takes work! It requires wisdom! *Is it worth it?*

one + one + One = ONE!

That answer on a math test would result in a failing grade. But that answer relative to our marriage would show great wisdom! That "math" is as old as time.

The marriage relationship is the first and most important relationship on earth. It is perfect, properly beautiful and epic in its original design. And regardless of whether your marriage right now is bad, average, good or great, the only destination worth pursuing is the one created before time even began, the one created by God!

Whatever your situation, our encouragement to you is that before you read further, stop and pray. Ask God to convict you that His desire and plan for your relationship is nothing short of epic and give you the revelation knowledge you need to step out in faith toward your destination of a properly beautiful marriage!

REFLECTION

Ask yourself the two foundational questions:
- On a scale of one to ten (ten being the best), how would you rate your marriage as it exists today?
- Are you content with your marriage? "Yes" or "no"?

Based on your answers, what does the journey ahead look like for you?
- Are you on the right path?
- Do you need to make a slight adjustment?
- Or do you need to completely change your vision of marriage and the path you are on?

CHAPTER 2

WHY MARRIAGE?

IF YOU WATCH A CARPENTER APPLY HIS or her skills to a project, it is easy to see that the good ones have the right tools for the job as well as the knowledge and experience of how to use them. Over the years, the technology of a carpenter's tools has changed drastically. At one point, every piece of wood was cut by hand—a slow and not so precise task. A man by the name of Edmond Michel is credited by many for inventing the electric circular saw in 1923. Today, this invention has drastically reduced the time involved in and improved the accuracy of cutting lumber.

There was a specific purpose Michel had in mind when he created his invention. But did you ever stop and think that a power saw could be used to cut your fingernails? When you are done laughing, you might recognize that it would work (at the cost of your fingertips). You could also realize that a two-by-four could be cut with fingernail clippers. Again, absurd but possible.

Those who choose to trim their nails with a circular saw would be considered to have what is referred to by some as a "spirit of stupid." Their alteration of the original creator's purpose is obviously foolish.

Having said that, there may be times when we "partner" with the original creator of something to improve its design or expand its use. I (Diane) often use the spin cycle of our washing machine to remove water from lettuce I have just washed. Still, the original purpose stays intact.

Many couples today attempt to improve upon and enhance God's original design and purpose of the marriage relationship. What we have to remember is that His original creation is perfect, and any attempt to improve it is foolish!

THE CREATOR

Both of us are blessed to sit in our different spaces each morning as we spend focused time with God. We can look out our respective windows, often as the sun is rising, and see a partial view of the lake we live near to, with the beautiful sky and trees reflecting off of the water. In those moments, it is easy to be grateful for the Creator and to be in awe of His creation.

When we are able to eliminate life's distractions for a moment, we can see God's handiwork all around us and marvel at His majesty. With the benefit of technological improvements, we can now see videos of the fascinating aquatic life on the ocean floor or watch documentaries on the universe and how the earth is the perfect distance from the sun so that we can survive physically. We both desire someday to see the aurora borealis and marvel at the colors God paints in the night sky.

Many have gazed up at a star-filled sky, away from the city lights, and tried to count how many there are. After a few seconds, there is the realization that it is an impossible task. (Some say it would take 10,000 years to count the stars in just our galaxy.) Yet God not only knows how many stars there are, but also "gives to all of them their names" (Psalm 147:4) because He created each one!

Each of us could easily spend an entire day writing about how amazing our Creator is in our eyes and praise Him for what He has created! But we would fall far short of capturing His "ability" because tomorrow—and every day through eternity—we continue to grow in our knowledge and understanding of God and His unconditional love for us.

As we reflect on God as Creator, we should keep in mind that all He has created is good (perfect, properly beautiful) and doesn't need changing. We should be humbled and amazed to remember that the One who created the sunset *chose* to create us, our spouse and the perfect relationship of marriage!

And He had a specific purpose for doing so!

THE PURPOSE

Mike's Story

I set a goal when I graduated from college to become a financial executive in a major corporation, believing that my value came from providing well for my family. Three distinct events happened that impacted my journey up the corporate ladder.

I met Diane and pursued her with everything I had until we married in 1979. Two and a half years later, our first daughter was born, and I became the sole provider for our family. I now had something worth the effort required to be successful in the corporate world, and that worth grew as our family expanded. It was part of my life's purpose.

A few months into our marriage, we both experienced God's unconditional love through individual weekend retreats, and it transformed our relationship with Jesus from servant to friend (see John 15:15). My focus in my work expanded to being a Godly man in the workplace (whatever that meant!) as well as a provider. It was another piece of my life's purpose—at least for a season.

The third event happened 25 years later when I was interviewing for a "bigger and better" CFO job. As I heard the CEO's answer to one of my questions, I realized that my corporate career was over: I had reached the career goal I had set when I started and had no desire to go any further. Soon after, my very successful position caused me great emotional and physical stress, and I knew something had to change. Fortunately, Diane was there to support me in the process.

Thus began my search for new direction…and new purpose.

While attending a leadership conference during my transition, I was greatly impacted when I heard the speaker, Dr. Howard Hendricks, make a statement that you should combine what you are good at, with what you like to do, with your passion, in order to find great joy and contentment in your career. As I prayed and processed through that concept with Diane, I came to the realization that my gifting, enjoyment and passion came from relationships. Every moment in the corporate world that brought me joy was from being significant in the lives of others—impacting them for good. Everything else, including the lie that my efforts were about being a good provider, was about *me* being successful.

I would be remiss if I didn't share that the transition over the next few years was difficult (but worthwhile). I continue to learn what it means to be authentic with myself, with God and with those in my inner circle of intimacy. I'm learning to better hear God and understand His purpose for creating me and creating marriage. I'm learning each day to choose His will and to walk with Him and Diane as one.

On this new path, I am continuing to learn what it looks like to be an epic husband, an epic father, an epic father-in-law, an epic grandfather and an epic coach/mentor/teacher. But the greatest discovery of all is the amazing joy that results whenever I am able to do it all for God's glory!

God's purpose and my purpose needed to be one and the same.

As we moved toward a new destination of a *properly beautiful* marriage, we realized we first needed to understand and reflect on God's *purpose(s)* for creating marriage.

One of the purposes we discovered is contained in Genesis 2 where God proclaims that it is not good for man to be alone. In the prior chapter, God creates man and then gives *them* dominion over the earth, so creating woman was not an afterthought—He already knew what was coming. But for what purpose?

Many of us assume that the woman was created in order for the man to *be* loved (and vice versa). Actually, the opposite is the truth. As Diane shared previously, she was focused on getting what she wanted out of marriage, not about giving. And I didn't know any better. So both of us were falling short of God's purpose and the resulting joy! Although it is a delight to be well loved, it is not our purpose. Each of us is created *to* love, not to be loved, and woman is the perfect object of man's affection (as he is hers) within the marriage relationship.

**God's design provides us a great opportunity *to* love.
It also provides a great opportunity to create.**

During our premarital counseling, our pastor suggested that we take some time to work on our relationship before we started a family. But if we weren't ready after a couple of years, he suggested we seek counsel to determine our direction. He knew that having children was a shared desire for us.

It was more than just a desire, as we believed a second part of God's purpose for our marriage was to "be fruitful and multiply and fill the earth and subdue it, and have dominion…" over all of it (Genesis 1:28). Because it was part of His purpose, we didn't take it lightly! Somewhere, somehow, we operated out of the wisdom that our purpose for having children was to expand God's Kingdom on earth by training up our children in the way they should go (Proverbs 22:6). They were not created for our happiness (that's called a pet), for our bidding (that's called a servant), or to glorify us. Rather, they were created to live as children of the King, for His glory.

Here again, there is nothing self-serving about this part of God's purpose for marriage. Rather, when we fulfill our purpose as parents, we live into what God intended and receive great joy as a result.

A third purpose for marriage we've figured out is that God wants us to understand and learn how to love and be loved unconditionally. The covenant relationship He created draws us into greater intimacy with each other as well as greater intimacy with Him. As Timothy Keller explains in his book *The Meaning of Marriage*, we will experience the fullness of the gospel as we live out God's design. And as we grow in our understanding of the gospel, our intimacy with each other (and with God) will continually increase. So will our intimacy with our own self.

Unconditional love makes it safe and beneficial for each of us to become more like our true self, knowing that our spouse won't leave, even though we're not the same person they married. (Thank God!)

In fact, as we become more Christ-like, they seem to adore us even more—and us them.

We have realized that…

As we mature in our faith, we grow in intimacy with God and mature in our role as a husband or wife. And as we mature as a husband or a wife, we grow in intimacy with each other.

It is humbling, and so fulfilling, when people "see" a joy in our relationship and want to know how to achieve that in their own marriage. Because therein lies a fourth purpose: to bring forth His glory, which we are created to do in everything. The apostle Paul tells us, "So, whether you eat or drink, or whatever you do, do all to the glory of God" (1 Corinthians 10:31). There is nowhere that this is truer than in living out our marriage vows! A marriage lived out of God's purpose reveals so much joy and goodness that observers "see" God in the individuals and the relationship.

God created the sacrament of marriage to provide someone for us to love, raise Godly children, teach us to love unconditionally, and bring forth His glory. This covenantal relationship that God created is properly beautiful.

Or at least it is supposed to be! What God created is *epic*! What the world has "recreated" falls way short of epic.

THE DESIGN

Diane's Story
Mike and I met in the corporate world. He was in accounting, and I was in finance. It was a world we knew and advanced in, believing in it to the point that we invested great time and energy into it. We both continued to learn by getting our MBAs. The only problem was, neither one of us was fulfilled by it.

I was relieved when we agreed that I should stay home to raise our kids, letting Mike continue to climb the corporate ladder.

Years later, he was invested quite deeply and growing more and more frustrated every day.

I knew how to be a corporate wife, which meant I came second to the job. That was okay as long as I had the possessions to show for my sacrifice. The day Mike came to me years later and said, "If I don't quit, I will die," was a scary day for many reasons. Of course, I wanted my husband to be healthy in body, mind and soul—but was I willing to agree to a significant change in our life—in my life?

This was not the man I married!

If our marriage was a contract, I could declare it void because I was no longer getting what I expected or agreed to. But if it was a covenant relationship, I had to look at things differently. Could I support my husband in order for him to take the time he needed to find and fulfill his purpose in life? Could I trust that God's plan for Mike would be good for me, our marriage and our family?

Was this change the "worse" of the "for better or worse" part of our covenant? Would the new season that resulted bring forth joy or despair? I had a choice. I could choose the life I had been accustomed to, or I could choose what was best for my husband and ultimately for my marriage—our marriage. I could choose to break the contract or stay committed to the covenant.

Through the counsel of our pastor, who taught us that "if it wasn't good for our marriage, it wasn't good for either one of us," we agreed it was worth the risk and effort to embark on a new path, one that was in the direction of an epic marriage.

God created covenant marriage. But what the world has recreated, and deceived the majority into living out, is contract marriage—which is practically a precursor to divorce. It is critical that we understand the difference and are honest in determining whether our marriage reflects a contract or a covenant.

What is the difference?

Most of us understand and have entered into a contract or two in our lifetime. We have reams of paper in our files from house and car purchases we've made together over the years. They formalize the commitments we made with other parties in which there was mutual agreement to provide the other with certain benefits: "If you do this for me, I will do that for you." The terms were clearly spelled out, and as long as both parties fulfilled their obligations, the contracts stayed intact until their intended expiration.

But there were options written into the contract that antici- pated one or both parties not living up to their end of the agree- ment, outlining the consequences if either party "broke" the agreement. And sometimes, rather than paying a penalty, peo- ple renegotiate a broken contract, with the result of having even more stringent terms (and a higher probability that the contract would be broken again).

Couples who enter into a contract marriage often find them- selves with "terms" that start out undefined and have a tendency to change as one or both partners desire something different. Marriage partners often find themselves expecting their spouse to meet their terms, even though their demands are selfish, unhealthy and unclear. The result is a broken contract. The "penalty" is dissolution of trust, lack of intimacy, loss of hope, bitterness and divorce.

When we say our wedding vows, regardless of the "promises" we make, if either spouse has his or her own best interest at heart, it is a two-party contract. And if either party has expectations that the spouse cannot, will not or should not meet, the "contract" is doomed from the start.

Now take it one step further. Since both parties have changed since their wedding day, their wants and needs have changed as well. So even if the terms of their marriage contract were clearly stated, agreed to and satisfied in the beginning, they are probably not being satisfied today.

That is man's recreation of God's original design—a contract marriage.

**God's original and perfect design
is for marriage to be a covenant!**

In their book *The Supernatural Ways of Royalty*, Kris Vallotton and Bill Johnson summarize a "true covenant" like this:

Covenant is comprised of three facets. First, it means an agreement that is only to be broken by death. Second, the nature of a covenant is that those who make it die to themselves for the sake of their covenant partner, and last, people who are in covenant give each other the right to influence their decisions. In other words, the focus of each member of the covenant is, "I'm in this relationship for what I can give to it, not just for what I can receive from it."[1]

When we understand and choose to enter into a covenant marriage, our hearts are focused on our spouse, with no escape clause. We also step into a three-part agreement: 1) each of us vowing to God that we agree that His plan is best and commit to following it; 2) each of us vowing to the other that we commit to fulfill His plan with him or her; and 3) God vowing with the two of us, as one, that we will now enter into His promise of great joy within this *properly beautiful* thing called marriage.

A contract marriage is self-focused, doesn't live out God's plan, is complicated and never attains epic proportions. A covenant marriage is spouse-focused, is what God created, is simple (not easy!) and when lived out, glorifies Him and brings great joy to you. It is epic!

Big difference!

THE REWARD

"His master said to him, 'Well done, good and faithful servant. You have been faithful over a little; I will set you over much. Enter into the joy of your master.'" (Matthew 25:23)

In Matthew's Gospel, Jesus shares what has become known as the parable of the talents (Matthew 25:14–30). A man is going on a journey and calls his servants together, giving each of them responsibilities commensurate with their abilities. Upon returning, he again calls them together to check on how well they have performed. The first two have done well and are given additional responsibility with great reward. The third chooses his own best interest and ends up with great loss.

How is that parable relevant in our marriage?

Understand that the "talents" given by the master to the servants represent what God has given to us (such as our monetary resources, giftings, anointing, etc.) and that we have a great responsibility to use them in ways that show forth His goodness and draw others to Him. God has also given us a great gift in the covenant of marriage, and we have a great responsibility to live it out in such a way that He is glorified and others are drawn to Him by observing us and seeing our joy!

And just like the servants in the parable, as we do, our responsibility will grow—with opportunities to reveal more of God—which will bring forth even greater reward. The reward is *joy*, but not just any joy. Rather, it is the same joy that God "experiences" constantly and forever.

When we choose to live out God's design for marriage with the one we have committed to live it with, we hear the words, "Well done! Enter into greater joy than you ever thought possible."

"There is a way that seems right to a man, but its end is the way to death." (Proverbs 14:12)

This wisdom from King Solomon is played out over and over every day in our world as we try to improve upon the already perfect creation of marriage.

God's creation of covenant marriage is perfect, created out of the overflow of His perfect love. He wants nothing more than to see our marriage become *perfectly beautiful*, expand His kingdom, fill us to overflowing with His unconditional love while we live out our purpose of loving our spouse the same way, and watch our joy be evident and contagious as we reveal His goodness in our epic marriage relationship.

REFLECTION

Think back to your wedding day and the vows that you made to each other as part of the ceremony.

- What were your expectations? Were they different than they are today?
- Did you enter into a contract or into a covenant?
- Does your marriage relationship today reflect a contract or a covenant?

If your marriage is a covenantal relationship, celebrate!

If it's a contractual agreement, know that through God's grace, your submission to His will, and some expert advice, it is never too late for it to be transformed into a covenant relationship.

In either case, keep reading, knowing that there is revelation ahead!

PART 2

INTIMACY—MY PART

CHAPTER 3

WHAT IS INTIMACY?

"MY WIFE THINKS I HAVE AN INTIMACY problem," the joke goes. "But she doesn't really know me." And therein lies the problem!

During our premarital counseling, we asked our pastor what he would recommend to start our marriage on a good path. He suggested that we each attend a faith renewal weekend, advertised as a three-day walk with Christ, that was happening shortly after our wedding. The idea sounded good until we realized we would be attending different weekends. How could something that separated us be good for our marriage? But off we went.

Diane's Story

Mike went first, leaving on Thursday evening and returning on Sunday. I heard nothing from him that entire weekend, which did not sit well with me. Plus, he "seemed" very different (not bad, just different) when he returned, making me wonder who I was married to.

By the time I left the following Thursday night, I was not a happy new wife. And despite the expectations of my husband and sponsors, I was determined that I would not come back different.

It didn't get any easier when I arrived, realizing that for three days I was expected to live with a group of women, none of whom I knew. The whole experience was growing more uncomfortable for me—and not just because of the cot they expected me to sleep on.

Friday morning, as I listened to the speakers talk very openly and vulnerably about their lives, the discomfort grew. I began looking for a way out—literally—and the retreat leaders began looking all over for me.

The pastor who found me wandering provided a great ear and great counsel as I poured out my heart. The prayers of the people praying for me 24/7, including my new husband, worked. I began to see God, others and myself in a different light.

I realized that I was not just trying to escape the retreat, but also myself. My struggle had to do with my fear of intimacy. I was trying to be who I thought I was supposed to be: the good girl who followed the commandments so God would love me. Due to my religious beliefs, I thought that I had to earn God's love, so I hid anything that I thought would be judged as wrong, convinced I could keep God from finding out. The truth was, I was trying to convince myself I was worthy of being loved by God, by myself and by others.

During that weekend, I learned that God *is* love and that I didn't have to earn it. I could stop living out of fear and start living an authentic life. This began my journey of growing in intimacy with myself and with God, so that I could experience deeper relationships with others, especially my husband. We had received good advice from our pastor!

Forty-five years later the journey continues. It is a lifelong process because we continue to change and evolve. We cannot hide from who we are or who we were created to be. Nor do we want to because our desire for intimacy grows with each new day.

INTIMACY DEFINED

A couple recently came in for counseling because they couldn't communicate with each other. We hear that complaint a lot, along with lack of affection, no common interests, finances or constant fighting—all signs of a lack of connection. A lot of these couples are just living as roommates and quickly agree that the critical element that is missing is *intimacy*.

Yet, how many of us understand what intimacy truly is? Although it is often thought of as a romantic replacement word for sex, it is so much more than that! We can simply say that *intimacy is a deep level of connection within a relationship*. But what does that really mean?

Are there different types of intimacy?
Is intimacy a need or a desire?
Is the need/desire different for a man versus a woman?
Do I have to share my emotions?
Can God's design for marriage exist without it?

Let's unpack that last question first.

In the beginning, God, *as the Trinity*, created the heavens, the earth and all living things. But He didn't "create" intimacy. That would mean intimacy didn't exist at one point. Rather, all that He created was created *out of* perfect intimacy. It is part of the essence of God. And since we were created in His image, it is part of our essence as well.

God's creation of marriage is no different. He declared that when a man and a woman enter into marriage, the two "shall become one" (Genesis 2:24). He designed marriage to be a beautiful relationship that reflects His essence—perfect intimacy!

God's design for marriage cannot exist without intimacy!

When we made the decision to pursue an epic marriage, it was because of the realization that our marriage wasn't perfect and, more so, that we were settling for less than perfection. However, making the decision didn't mean that suddenly our marriage was perfect. Rather, it meant that our marriage journey was now pointed toward that goal. We needed knowledge and wisdom to move in the direction of perfect intimacy, so we started to explore some of those other questions, trying to understand *what* intimacy was.

Different Types of Intimacy

Jesus modeled intimacy for us in His relationships. He had many friends and followers, but His relationship seemed to be different with Peter, James and John, with His mother and with Mary, Martha and Lazarus. The type of intimacy changed with each connection.

The five types most commonly referred to are:

1. **Emotional:** *Honestly sharing our feelings, thoughts and beliefs and our dreams and fears.*

Throughout our marriage, we have made a point of getting away together for a few days at least once a year, just the two of us. Without the distractions of everyday life, we are able to really share what's on our hearts and hear what is on each other's heart. It's when we allow ourselves to really dream and become united in each other's dreams. We share our gratitude for our family, our work and so much more! We laugh even more than usual and celebrate our oneness.

2. **Spiritual:** *Exploring our inner beliefs, values and philosophical views and finding truth together.*

Our family dinners with our daughters and their families are a time of great joy—there is lots of laughter and tears as we share the blessings and struggles of life as well as what God is revealing in the process. It is a safe place to process our deepest spiritual thoughts and marvel at the majesty of God and how He is working in our marriages, parenting, careers and creative projects.

As a couple, our individual times of intimacy with God spill over into great conversations with each other, uniting both our hearts and His.

3. **Intellectual:** *Being safe to voice our opinions, thoughts, ideas and interests.*

Since the beginning of our relationship, we have valued each other's thoughts and opinions on pretty much everything. We both love to learn, and as the seasons of life have changed, so have the topics of our conversation. In the early years, there were a lot of conversations about raising children and finances. Today, a lot are about human behavior and health. Even when there was tension due to a difference of opinion, we seldom lost sight of the opportunity to grow in knowledge through each other's thoughts and ideas.

This is perhaps the most difficult type of intimacy to experience these days because people often use social media to voice their opinion, often without allowing others to share theirs. Intellectual intimacy only exists within an environment of mutual respect and open communication. But it also requires us to have a desire to seek truth, which we can find faster together than alone.

4. Social: *Spending time together and experiencing common interests.*

I (Mike) am an avid golfer. What I realized through years of experience is that I would rather have an average round with good friends than a great round with people I don't know or enjoy. (No comment on the bad rounds!)

A lot of our intimate social gatherings are with family and friends we are intimate with in other areas. Some are with neighbors we only connect with socially. What makes the gatherings enjoyable is when the conversation goes deeper than the weather or our ailments!

5. Physical: *Affectionately touching and physically connecting (both sexually and non-sexually).*

There is a scene in the movie *Phenomenon* where the character Lace washes and cuts George's hair. We realize the characters are actors acting, but it is a great depiction of what physical intimacy looks like.

God's design for marriage incorporates a great deal of purpose for physical intimacy, both sexual (which is a chapter in itself) and non-sexual. We choose to hold hands when we're walking, and we sit next to each other on the couch when we're watching television. We make sure that our kids and grandkids don't walk away from our time together without a hug and kiss good-bye. It is both a need and a desire for them and for us!

The stories we read about Jesus' life reveal that He had a strong emotional connection with Peter, James and John that didn't exist to the same degree with His other followers. With Mary, Martha and Lazarus, He likely had a strong social connection that went back years before He met and called any of His disciples. And certainly He had a strong emotional connection with His mother. But there was also a high degree of physical connection with her since she gave birth to Him, nourished Him and comforted Him as a child when He skinned His knee.

Jesus modeled intimacy in His relationships, including being selective with an inner circle. Like us, He would have been emotionally exhausted if He had tried to share His thoughts and feelings beyond that smaller group.

Our relational connections are designed to be limited—with a few close friends, with our family and certainly with God. Often, we have more than one type of intimacy with a friend or relative (except sexual). But our relationship with our spouse must include all five types to claim perfect intimacy.

> **For a marriage to approach epic,
> it *must* have all five types of intimacy.**

AN INHERENT NEED AND DESIRE

Intimacy: A Need or Desire?
The answer is yes!

Our youngest grandchild will put his arms up to be held by one of his parents or us, his grandparents, when he meets someone new. He desires to be held because that is how he satisfies his need to feel safe. Very rarely do we have an inherent need without a corresponding desire to go along with it.

Our bodies need nutrition through food and water, and our hunger pains and thirst drive us to desire to eat and drink. We need rest, and when we are tired, we desire to crawl into bed and fall asleep. An infant who is consistently held will physically grow at a healthier rate than one who isn't. Babies need intimacy. They will often cry even when their diaper is dry and they're well fed. It is their way of expressing their desire to be held.

Security, control and affection are inherent needs. Intimacy falls under the affection category. More and more studies are reporting the physical benefits of healthy relationships: elevated immunity, longer lives, less depression/anxiety, etc. We *need* intimacy to maintain our physical and emotional health.

At the same time, although we can survive without intimacy, when a piece is missing, our quality of life suffers. Years ago we were at a family gathering, reliving memories with relatives, including one of Diane's uncles. He had lost his wife more than 20 years earlier to cancer and had done a great job of caring for himself and his family, both physically and emotionally. But we could see a sadness wash over him as he talked about her and shared stories of their time together. The one thing he hadn't been able to replace in his life was the intimacy that existed in their marriage relationship. Twenty years later, the desire for it still existed.

**God created us to need intimacy to survive
and to desire intimacy to thrive!**

The Need for Intimacy: Man vs. Woman

A common statement is that men spell intimacy S-E-X and women spell it T-A-L-K! We will explore this idea in greater detail in a later chapter, but it contains a lot of truth. We *are* different! That's the way God designed it to be. We are different in nature, temperament, emotions and emotional responses—which means that when it comes to intimacy, most men and women approach it differently.

Often what's not obvious is how the heart of a man and the heart of a woman influences that difference. Part of studying each other and growing in deeper understanding is acknowledging, accepting and appreciating our natural design.

We realized that truth one day at the end of a great, but intense, conversation about our relationship. As we sat on the swing overlooking the lake in our neighborhood, we were well connected. Then we had a great laugh when "one of us" said to the other, "You want to go have sex now, don't you?" Which was true! And it helped us both realize that a man and a woman experience the fullness of intimacy differently.

We researched the natural differences between men and women when we were developing a marriage workshop. It was very eye-opening, extremely valuable and sometimes amusing to gain greater understanding of each other's—and our own—inner workings. It was also sometimes confusing and raised the questions of "why" and "what." Why did God make us this way? What do we do with the knowledge regarding our own behavior and our response to our spouse's behavior?

The answer? We openly share and we intently listen. *We communicate!*

The wisdom we gain when we do so is critical and will grow as we gain intimacy with our own self, with God and with our spouse.

Men and women don't think alike
because they're not supposed to!

Sharing Emotions

I (Mike) struggled with a sensitive spirit when I was growing up. I was often teased by family and friends when tears rolled down my cheeks and was accused of being "too sensitive." I eventually learned it was a gift, but not before I developed some unhealthy behavior around it. Not only did I stop sharing my emotions out of the fear of being rejected, but I also created an unsafe environment for others to share theirs. The level of emotional intimacy that Diane and I now have in our relationship took a lot of self-reflection, effort and risk, but it has resulted in great connection.

When it comes to emotional intimacy, we have to have the goal of being all in, which requires taking a big risk! When we share our opinions or decisions, we run the risk of being rejected. But when we share our emotions, the risk of rejection goes to a much higher level. It is a lot more painful to have our feelings denied than to have someone disagree with our opinions.

Women are better at sharing emotions than men, probably because culture has taught us that lie. In a marriage relationship, both must openly share their feelings and allow the other to safely share his or hers as well.

We limit our risk of rejection by not sharing
our emotions—but at the expense of intimacy!

We may never fully understand why we were created to be different than our spouse. Perhaps our Creator knew being different would require us to have a deep understanding of our own self and each other, require us to openly share our needs and desires, and to pursue each other's joy.

In all cases, we need to realize that intimacy is both a need and a desire; it requires self-awareness and authenticity; it means we must be transparent as well as vulnerable; it involves deep understanding; it is something we must intentionally seek; it is different for a man than it is for a woman; and it must include all five types...

...in order for our marriage to grow into a properly beautiful relationship of intimacy.

REFLECTION

Think about three people in your life, other than your spouse, with whom you have a close relationship.

- How well do you think they really know you?
- What part of you do you hold back from them?
- What is the fear that keeps you from sharing that part of you with them?

Now answer the same questions relative to your relationship with your spouse.

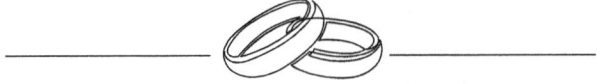

CHAPTER 4

FINDING INTIMACY

"RECALCULATING..."

Our youngest daughter, Molly, had a great opportunity to spend a year studying in Florence, Italy. She was a wonderful tour guide when we went to visit her. But we would have been lost without our Garmin GPS system as we explored the countryside. I lost count of how many times we heard it say that word: "*Recalculating*."

Dorothy was lucky—she had a yellow brick road to follow to get to the Emerald City!

In our touring Italy, and in the case of Dorothy trying to get back to Kansas, there was a destination. Sort of. But it was what transpired through the journey that created the greatest value.

Based on a true story, the movie *Remember the Titans* is a great example of how we are transformed through the path we take to find our way. A group of individuals, thrown together through forced integration, reap great success as a high school football team. However, although the success of winning a state championship was achieved (the destination), it was the journey—the bonding together of lives and the life lessons—that created the real joy.

Both the players and the coaches learned the importance of becoming a team by individually being transparent and vulnerable, appreciating each other's value and role, and by individually and together seeking after oneness.

Intimacy is our destination. And by understanding what it looks like, we'll know when we arrive. Like the football team in the movie, the journey will be both challenging and life-changing. But what path do we follow to get there?

When we were developing a vision for our counseling/ministry center, we knew that our primary focus was intimacy. We knew that it included intimacy with our own self, with God and with others. We spent a lot of hours discussing whether our relationship with God or with self comes first—not in importance, but in progression. We eventually adopted the idea that intimacy with our own self is necessary in order to enhance intimacy with God, knowing that both are critical to create and maintain an intimate relationship with others.

IT STARTS WITH ME

It is often very difficult when counseling others to get them to talk about father (or mother) wounds. The immediate response is usually, "Oh, I had great parents!" That might be true, but....

Mike's Story

I had the same reaction when someone asked me that question.

At a men's retreat, years into our marriage and my spiritual journey, the speaker directed us to prayerfully discern a father wound. Then we were to determine what lie we believed as a result, any vows that we made, and the behavior we adopted from the vow.

The thought that immediately came into my mind was that I didn't have any, just as the speaker encouraged those who didn't think they had any to give the exercise a chance. Within 30 seconds of asking the Holy Spirit for enlightenment, I was overcome with a father wound I had been carrying for over 40 years.

I didn't truly know or understand what true intimacy looked like!

My dad was a man of few words all of his life. He loved and cared deeply, but he seldom expressed his feelings out loud, especially in my younger years. I cherished the notes and letters he sent me over the years because he was great at revealing his heart through writing. That, along with great hugs, seemed like enough.

So when the revelation came that we didn't have deep, intimate conversations during my formative years—during the time I was trying to figure out what being a man was supposed to look like—there was a deep sadness I experienced for both myself and for him.

It was easy to recognize where his inability to be intimate came from. He lost his mom at the age of ten, got kicked out of the parochial school because his dad couldn't pay for his mom's funeral, ended up with a wicked stepmother shortly thereafter when his dad married a woman to help him take care of four boys, and then left home at 18 to fend for himself. His dad, a first-generation immigrant from Italy in a strange country with an unfamiliar language, was also a man of few words.

My dad's difficult early life kept me from learning by example the importance of being intimate! As I experienced the knowledge of that wound and reflected on its impact, I had an even greater revelation that greatly changed my life.

Knowing that my earthly father is to be a model for my heavenly Father, I realized I had a warped view of God. Like Diane, I had grown up experiencing the religious teaching of having to earn God's love. The reason I came back different from the weekend she mentioned earlier is that I experienced Jesus in relationship, not just in knowledge. But because of the example I learned from my dad, I still saw my heavenly Father as distant and unapproachable. When I realized that wasn't true and renounced the lie that He didn't want to have deep intimate conversations with me, my communion with God blossomed.

I'm grateful for the revelation I received that weekend and the understanding that intimacy is something I both need and desire—and that it starts with *me*.

Intimacy is often stated as "in-to-me-see." It's a creative play on the word itself, and it does contain an important truth: you must be aware of who you are before you can openly share yourself with God or your spouse. Our job when counseling individuals or couples is to help them understand what they really believe, identify those beliefs that are unhealthy, and then guide them toward adopting the healthy beliefs they choose.

And whereas intimacy with our own self and with God is available just as we are, intimacy with another often first requires refinement in both parties' beliefs and actions.

WE MUST DECIDE TO BE TRANSPARENT, VULNERABLE AND AUTHENTIC

We throw around the words *transparency, vulnerability* and *authenticity* without often understanding their meaning. A good friend shared this thought one day: transparency is sharing who you really are with someone, and vulnerability is allowing that person to speak into your transparency.

Initially, a great deal of our time with our clients is spent creating an environment where they trust that they won't be judged and that what they reveal will be held in confidence. Only then will they open up to us by sharing a life experience, fear, mistakes, etc. That's transparency. In that sharing, often the real issue surfaces. Because they have decided to trust us, they allow us to process that with them and seek our advice. That's vulnerability.

But that is still not intimacy, unless it's authentic (that is, completely honest) and *is reciprocated*.

In our 45 years of marriage, we have learned a great deal about each other, but the greatest understanding—growth toward intimacy—has been in the times when we have been fully transparent in our dreams, our wounds, our sadness and our joy and then allowed the other to partner with us in that. Again, that sharing, listening and intentionally trying to understand each other is *communication*!

Our hearts and minds must be totally revealed and blended together in order to experience the beauty of intimacy.

There is a scene in the movie *Good Will Hunting* where Sean, the therapist, is making a point to his client that love and intimacy with someone is about accepting the quirks and peculiar habits that only are discovered through the pursuit of deep understanding. Regarding his wife who has died, Sean says, "...those are the things I miss the most—the little idiosyncrasies that only I know about. That's what made her my wife."[1]

The relationship between husband and wife is the most important one on earth. Doesn't it make sense then that there should be things about each other—those idiosyncrasies—that the two only share with each other? That's what makes one the spouse!

**"I love that about you. And I love
that I am the only one who does."**

Gaining understanding of ourselves and our spouse does not create intimacy unless we intentionally *seek after it*. On our wedding day, if we had written down what we thought our marriage life was going to look like, it would have included long walks holding hands, deep conversations in front of the fireplace, tender lovemaking in front of that same fireplace, praying together, holding our newborn, our family sitting around the kitchen table eating dinner or playing a board game, laughter, tears of joy and comforting each other in times of loss. Like most couples starting out, our vision was a relationship of perfect intimacy.

What wouldn't have been on our list was falling asleep on the couch watching TV, having to share a bathroom, working overtime, eating fast food on the way to soccer practice, having arguments, walking in late for church, dealing with financial stress, etc.

For most of us, when our life spins out of control, we blame it on the demands of the day and age we are living in! And although we can't always control life's circumstances, it is also true that we most often choose those things that make our life about doing rather than being.

What if, instead, we chose to make intimacy a top priority? If spending quality time with our family was more important than a big house, would we choose a less demanding job? If deep conversation was more important than the ball game or reality show, would we spend more time around the dinner table? If date night was the highlight of our weekly calendar, would we leave the office on time? Would the laughter and tears of joy pour forth? Would we cling to each other and pray in a time of loss? Would our marriage exceed our wildest dreams, or at least encompass what we originally imagined?

Intimacy is not contained in one of the packages on the gift table at our wedding reception. We must strive for it, we must search for it, and we must cling to it when we find it.

Intimacy is a gift that must be opened over and over.

Intimacy with our own self, with God and with others is discussed individually in the chapters ahead with the understanding that growth in one positively impacts growth in the others. For now, we need to grasp this:

Intimacy comes from a relationship with a deep level of connection with our own self, with our Creator and with our spouse. Because it has always been a part of our essence, our work *is to understand it, develop it, unleash it and celebrate it!*

Intimacy *is* a gift, to both ourselves and to our spouse. We must choose over and over to do the work necessary to more clearly reflect who we were created to be as an individual and as a partner in marriage. We must allow and encourage each other to do the same. And, although we must maintain the focus on the destination of intimacy with self, God and others, we should also appreciate the journey, through which we will experience the greatest benefit.

REFLECTION

Think on these questions:
- What "little idiosyncrasies" does your spouse know about you that no one else does?
- What "little idiosyncrasies" do you know about your spouse that no one else does?

Reflect on your connection with yourself, with God and with your spouse.

- How well do you really know yourself?
- How authentic are you when you spend time connecting with God?
- How well do you know your spouse and how well does he or she know you?

CHAPTER 5

It Begins with Me

"Do not be conformed to this *world, but be trans-formed by the renewal of your mind, that by testing you may discern what is the will of God, what is good and acceptable and perfect.*" (Romans 12:2)

There's a parable we heard once from somewhere that goes like this:

A man makes an appointment with a lawyer because he is extremely unhappy in his marriage. His wife is not living up to her end of their so-called contract. When he sits down across from the attorney, his bitterness is obvious. The lawyer asks him to describe his issues and frustrations, and the man doesn't hold back.

When he's finished berating his wife, the lawyer asks him if he would really like to stick it to her. And of course, the husband answers yes. "Here's my recommendation," says the wise attorney. "For the next 30 days, make her think she's the most important person in the world. Tell her often that she's beautiful, that she's a great mom, how much you appreciate how she manages the house and cares for you. Bring her flowers and gifts and affectionately greet her in the morning when you get up and again when you arrive back home in the evening."

The husband, a little confused, asks why he would do that. The attorney says that after 30 days, they can serve the wife with divorce papers and that she will be very surprised and devastated by the husband's request based upon how he has been treating her.

The husband's eyes light up as he recognizes the evil in the lawyer's plan, and he quickly agrees. For the next 30 days, he does exactly as the attorney recommends—and his wife is delighted to experience this change in her husband's attitude and behavior.

After 30 days, he returns to the lawyer's office and, when asked how it went, says, "Perfect!" The attorney nods as he pulls the divorce papers out of his drawer. "Are you ready to sign the papers and destroy her world?" he asks.

The husband responds, "Why would I want to do that? I'm married to the most wonderful woman in the world!"

I HAVE MET THE ENEMY, AND IT IS ME!

It is amazing how our thoughts and emotions are transformed when we change our filter!

Often a couple enters marriage thinking it means "*I'm* the 'one,' and my spouse must become like me," with the expectation that the other person is going to change. When the change doesn't occur, resentment rises, followed by a decision that they are wrong for each other—and the marriage ends. A common theme is, "We just grew apart, and he (or she) won't change, so I'm done trying to make this work."

It is devastating and so contrary to God's design when a couple becomes this hardened and hateful towards each other. They progress from self-pity to resentment to bitterness to anger to retaliation to hatred and finally to divorce. In the path of that, many lives are destroyed and hearts broken.

Often it is at this point that a couple will come to counseling to make a last-ditch effort, not so much to save the marriage as to say they did everything they could before giving up. Each one wants a witness who will say he or she was right and the spouse was wrong.

We try to help them understand that it's not about one's being right and the other wrong; it's more about them being different. And if they start to understand and embrace their differences (at least the healthy differences), their marriage could survive and even become great. But it starts with them individually. How are their own behaviors causing problems for themselves, their spouse and for their marriage?

The goal is to help both of them become self-aware of their own identity—who they are, who they were created to be, and whether they will choose to change—and, in the process, change their filter so that they can understand and appreciate their spouse's identity and the work the spouse is choosing to do as well.

WHAT'S MY STORY?

I (Mike) spoke at a men's breakfast one morning on the topic of identity. On the left side of a large white board, I listed those things about me that you would find on a profile: the color of my hair and eyes, whether I was male or female, my age, nationality, the town I grew up in, etc. On the right side of the board, I listed some of my life events, some accomplishments, some great memories and some difficult experiences. I explained to the group that the list on the left described me while the list on the right defined me.

We will share more about the purpose of the teaching in a subsequent chapter, but the process of creating the lists was very enlightening. Capturing your identity on paper or creating a timeline can be very enlightening in the process of focusing on intimacy with one's self, or "self-intimacy."

How well do you know yourself? Just for fun, take a sheet of paper and write down as many words that you can think of that describe you—*in one minute.*

If your list includes ten words or more, then you did better than 75% of those who have done this exercise in the past. Part of the reason the lists are so short is because of the time pressure. But, more realistically, we often have a limited understanding of our identity because we seldom take the time to think about it.

Our list may include the color of our eyes or hair or that we are male or female—words that describe our *natural traits/characteristics* that we are born with and have no influence over. Some of our

43

natural traits are unique, such as our physical features, while others are thought to be inherent in us all, such as our ability to smile, count, communicate and react to danger.

God created men and women to have natural differences as well—often for reasons we don't understand. There's a great YouTube clip, "It's Not About the Nail" by Jason Headley, that humorously illustrates this difference. We won't give away the plot, but let's just say that most men and women will respond "yep" when they see it. In real life, I (Diane) had a wife in a counseling session say to me once, "Sometimes I just want an 'aw, honey.'" When I asked her what that was, she said, "It's when my husband just puts his arms around me and says, 'Aw, honey, I hear you, and I'm so sorry that you are hurting.' He doesn't try to fix it, but rather just shares my frustration."

Men and women are also different in the way we process information. Think of it in terms of a laptop with multiple programs and apps. A woman's screen is likely to have multiple windows open all at once, each one representing something that needs attention: the kids, career, the home, what's for dinner and so on. And although each task may be partially minimized on the screen, it stays active until there is some resolution or at least a plan on what to do.

For men, there is one window open at a time. They are able to focus on one thing and let go of everything else. That app gets closed, or at least fully minimized, before they move on to another topic or issue.

Despite gender research now saying that neither men nor women are good at multitasking, women in general just have a harder time letting go of unresolved responsibilities.

If we don't appreciate that difference between ourselves and our spouse, then it is difficult for a man to understand why a woman is so stressed out all the time and a woman to understand how a man can just sit on the couch when there is so much to do and so much to think about!

We figured out early in our marriage that weekend getaways were important so that we could work together to close many of the open windows and prioritize our "marriage window." (By the way, it worked best when I planned and organized the weekend so that Diane didn't have to open another window!)

Then there are our physical differences. Those may not be unique in the sense that we may have the same eye color as our spouse. But there are many physical differences between a man and a woman—some of which are obvious and some are not.

The way we process information, our physical makeup, our personality and our gifting are part of our natural characteristics...

...and our *natural differences* are neither wrong nor right; they're just different. But it's important that we understand them and how they impact us, especially as we go through the different seasons of our lives.

Our list from the exercise described earlier may also include our habits, preferences and behaviors. This part of our identity is influenced by our environment or by what we have been taught—our *learned behaviors and traits.*

Scientists generally agree that our athletic ability is influenced by our DNA (because of our *natural* body type, reflexes and explosive power, etc.) but a great athlete has also *learned* how to strengthen the right muscles, eat the right foods and practice the right drills. So, we (and those we have learned from) have influence over a large part of our identity and whether our behavior is healthy or unhealthy.

It is the *learned behaviors/traits* that we need to become more aware of. What are they? Are they healthy or unhealthy? And where did they come from?

We took our grandkids out for pizza one afternoon, and as we were leaving, our nine-year-old grandson stopped to hold the door for a woman walking out behind us. We could tell she was surprised by his gentlemanly behavior as well as by his polite response when she said thank you. No one ever intentionally taught Harry to hold the door for another person. It was just something he had learned was the right thing to do by observing others' behavior and response.

Much of our *learned behavior* comes through the instruction of parents, teachers, pastors and friends or through what we read. But what we observe and experience, healthy and unhealthy, is even more powerful. If we participate in a game of Simon Says, we're most likely to *do* what the leader is doing rather than what he or she is saying!

Learned behaviors are often deeply ingrained in us and hard to change because of how we learned them and who taught us those behaviors.

One of our spiritual mentors taught us that "Jesus trumps culture"—an important truth. Contained in that truth is also the idea that we have *cultural differences*. These may often be thought of as natural behaviors, but our culture plays a significant role in our learned behavior.

One of the highlights of the trip we took to Italy was visiting the village where my (Mike's) grandmother grew up. Because it was still in the family, we were able to explore the actual house that Nonna grew up in. The emphasis of *famiglia* (family) in the Italian culture was highlighted by the layout of the house. On the ground floor, there were three kitchens, each with its own living room space, while upstairs there were multiple bedrooms and a couple of bathrooms that were shared. Three different related families lived together—and generation after generation, that cultural norm continued. It carried into my childhood as well, as I spent almost every Sunday dinner at Nonna and Nonno's house with all of my cousins.

Cultural differences can be as extreme as coming from different countries or as simple as coming from different neighborhoods. It often determines the language we speak, the food we eat and the music we listen to. It can also determine how we greet someone (a handshake, a bow or a kiss on the cheek), celebrate holidays and even our punctuality.

Because our cultural traits are learned, some are healthy while others are not. We worked with a couple where one of them was consistently late whenever they went out socially. That spouse's ethnic culture had taught that arrival time wasn't important. To this individual it was a way of life. But to the spouse it was disrespectful. When they recognized that their difference came from their culture and not disrespect, they came to an agreement that worked for their marriage.

Many couples struggle every year to satisfy their families' traditions related to the celebration of holidays. A joyful time ends up stressful and unappreciated, and so creating new traditions and memories for their own immediate family never happens.

Because I (Diane) also grew up in a culture that appreciated family mealtime, it was, and still is, something that is highly regarded in our family today. However, my childhood culture wasn't driven by nationality; rather, it was the choice of my parents to make this a part of our immediate family culture.

Family meals together usually represent a healthy culture. There are also unhealthy family cultures that we bring into our marriage. For example, there are productive and unproductive ways to resolve conflict. When we ask couples struggling with resolving conflict what their conflict resolution process is, they will most likely say, "We don't have one." But they do! And it is most often the process they learned from watching their parents, which is different than what their spouse learned from their parents—neither of which was effective. The unhealthy styles they learned through family culture resulted in bitterness and exhaustion because issues remain unresolved and come up over and over.

I (Mike) could tell when my parents were fighting because my dad would give my mom the silent treatment. I carried that culture into our marriage by doing the same to Diane. I don't know if my dad ever realized how destructive and controlling that was, but I knew it—and still did it—because it was deeply ingrained in me. Through self-realization and counsel, I changed an unhealthy family culture.

Our *cultural differences* greatly impact our relationship, so we need to understand how our culture has influenced us individually and appreciate the healthy traits (in ourselves and our spouse) while working to change the unhealthy ones—for the good of the marriage!

That spiritual mentor we mentioned before used to say, "We all have garbage we bring into our marriage. Mine doesn't stink to me, and my spouse's doesn't stink to him or her. But when we combine the two piles, it now stinks to both of us."

All of us have baggage we carry throughout our lives as an open wound, or if we've done the healing work, as a scar that reminds us of what we went through. This comes from experiences such as abandonment, betrayal, abuse and other forms of trauma that affect our self-esteem and cause an identity crisis. It also comes from decisions we make to mask the pain of that trauma.

Often we hide that baggage from others—and maybe even ourselves—because of shame, and we come into a relationship unaware or unable to share who we truly are.

It is usually through individual counseling that we are able to identify the wound and begin the healing process. In a marriage relationship, if our wounds are not identified and healed, we are often triggered by our spouse, resulting in conflict and unhealthy behavior.

For example, someone who has abandonment issues might accuse a spouse of having an affair if he or she is late getting home from work. The innocent spouse will be blindsided by this accusation, and the lack of trust by each of them could lead to bitterness, anger and even divorce—all because the abandonment wound had never been identified and healed.

We both brought baggage into our relationship, some of which we didn't even know existed. And without dealing with it, our marriage would have been in great danger of not achieving intimacy.

Diane's Story

I had a really hard time if Mike was ever late picking me up from somewhere. It didn't matter if there was good reason or not, or that it was a rare experience. My first thought was, "he doesn't value me," and conflict would ensue.

As we learned the importance of identifying our wounds and processing through them, I did just that. I figured out that the source of my hurt was from a childhood wound. Each time Mike was late, it (subconsciously) reminded me of the memory of sitting on the school steps as a ten-year-old, waiting for my "ride."

My parents operated a small resort that we called home, and some of the workers were like family. They often were my ride, and on occasion they would get distracted for a few minutes, causing them to be late. The memory I formed was that it happened a lot, that I was all alone sitting on those steps, and that my parents didn't care about me. All lies! Which I figured out when I became transparent and vulnerable in dealing with it.

What I now believe is that it rarely happened, that there were always other people around (including supervisors) so I was never unsafe, and that when my parents found out about it, they worked to correct the situation. They greatly valued me!

That wound—my baggage—can still be triggered. I still have a hard time if Mike is late. And my first thought can still be that he doesn't value me. But I have learned to address the lies that might surface and replace them with the truth.

I'm not alone in my "work." Because Mike does greatly value me, he does all that he can to be on time. And if there is an occasion when he is late, he doesn't make excuses, and he validates my feelings.

Through our pursuit of intimacy, we have gained great understanding.

WHAT'S MY VALUE SYSTEM?

Our natural traits, cultural differences, learned behaviors and baggage all contribute to what is defined as our *value system*. It is the total of all of our ideas and beliefs and how important each one is to us. It includes every opinion we have about life. It is developed by what we have been taught, along with our experiences and what we have learned through them, and our corresponding response.

Our value system is unique. It is shaped by our moral code, which often aligns with that of others (and hopefully with our spouse's). But it also includes our unique preferences for things like seasons or hobbies—preferences that do not deal with morals—and will not completely align with our spouse's. It seldom takes more than three questions before a difference in two people's value system is identified.

Regardless of whether our eyes are blue or that we slurp our soup, in the famous words of that cartoon philosopher Popeye: "I yam what I yam." Popeye acknowledged who he was despite all of his shortcomings. Are you able to say that about yourself?

Knowing our story starts with looking genuinely at who we are right now. What is our filter? Then we can move

toward understanding who we were created to be—and how to get there—through *the renewal of our mind and changing our filter!*

Moving toward an epic marriage begins with us individually as we gain knowledge and understanding of our natural traits, cultural differences, learned behaviors and the baggage we carry. Knowing our story, how it developed and its impact on us and others will lead us to a place where we can determine what it could and should look like going forward. We can choose to change that part that is unhealthy.

When our spouse does the same and we gain understanding of each other's value system and how it developed, we can be encouragers to each other through this process of refinement.

REFLECTION

Spend some prayerful time thinking about your behaviors. Can you think of a few that are healthy as well as some that aren't?

Reflecting on these behaviors...

- When did they begin and what opinion or belief drives them?
- Is the motivation for those behaviors a result of fear or desire?
- Do you want to change those unhealthy behaviors?

Continue to the next chapter to learn how to upgrade your value system in order to choose behaviors that are healthy for you and for others.

CHAPTER 6

A NEW VISION

IMAGINE A ROOM FULL OF PEOPLE SPLIT into two sides. Those on the right side of the room are given glasses with clear lenses, and those on the left are given glasses with lenses that are tinted blue. Then someone holds up a lemon in front of the group.

When asked to describe the object, both groups agree that the object is oval or oblong in shape, is two to three inches long, and has a bump or bulge at one end. They all even acknowledge that the object is a member of the citrus family—a fruit.

But when asked to specifically name the piece of fruit, the two sides disagree. The group on the right correctly identifies it as a lemon. But the group on the left identifies it as a lime. The yellow color of the fruit plus their blue-tinted glasses results in their seeing the object as being the color green.

Both sides are confident in their answer. The side that correctly identifies the object as a lemon has no distortion of the facts and clearly sees the truth. The side whose view is distorted swears that the object is a lime and cannot see the truth until they remove their blue-tinted glasses, which distort the truth.

We spend a great deal of our life looking at ourselves and others (that is, our spouse) through glasses that distort the truth. The image in the mirror is what we truly believe, but it is often blurry or totally inaccurate because of the filters we have "put on" through false teaching and difficult life experiences. It is an intentional and lifelong process to deal with our filters so that we can see our authentic self and walk out our true identity.

Through awareness, conviction and refinement, we can begin to see who we really are and move toward the image of who God created us to be.

UNDERSTANDING AND APPRECIATING OUR UNIQUENESS

It's a beautiful thing that our value systems are unique. Again, it's part of God's creative genius. And it is true that we are who we are because of all of our ideas and beliefs, our desires, our behavior and the priority we give to each. Being intimate with our own self helps us to continually ask ourselves, "Why do I think, feel and act the way I do?"

What is often misunderstood is that our mind, our affections and our will are *one* system in us. Our minds inform our affections of what will bring us the greatest happiness; our affections create a desire for it; and our will chooses to pursue it. All three work together, starting with our mind (our thoughts, beliefs, understanding, memory, judgement, discernment and conscience). But it is often the understanding of our emotions that provides insight into what we are thinking. Meanwhile, our choices can steer us to know how we truly feel.

Sometimes it's simple. Our daughters are six years apart. Our oldest, Katie, had a great wardrobe that most little girls would adore. So of course, I (Diane) saved it all for Molly. The only problem was that Molly knew herself so well, even as a little girl, that she let me know, "Those clothes might be your style, Mom, but they're not mine!" How ironic that Molly ended up majoring in fashion design in college!

Other times we have to dig a little to understand our values. We had a small conflict we discovered early in our marriage. Sometimes I (Mike) liked to take a nap on the couch on a Sunday afternoon. But Diane was confused and somewhat frustrated by that because "you only took naps when you were sick!"

Sunday afternoon naps were a regular occurrence for Mike's family. But I (Diane) experienced my dad taking naps as he was fighting cancer. Each of us had a different mindset because of the emotion we experienced growing up.

What is also important to understand is that we must *continually* do the self-intimacy work required to really know ourselves, know who we are created to be, and move in that direction.

Often a husband or wife will complain that his or her spouse has changed. "He (or she) is not the person I married." Our response is, "He (or she) is not supposed to be." What's important is whether the change is healthy or unhealthy.

Mike's Story

Remember the story of the men's breakfast meeting that I shared earlier? The list of things on the left side of the whiteboard that described me has not really changed (except my hair is now gray instead of brown). But the life events that I wrote on the right side of the whiteboard—the list that defines me—has expanded. And because every day involves new experiences, good and difficult, I have to continually look at myself in the mirror to determine who I am today.

I was sharing on the topic of identity—how our life experiences change us and mold us, depending on our response to them. There were a number of traumatic events I talked about, and I expressed how grateful I was that the grace of God transformed me (I think in a good way) through them.

One man came up to me afterwards and said he was jealous because he had not experienced any significant loss in his life. We had a great conversation about the irony of his emotion. It was not that he wanted to experience tragedy, but rather he longed for the transformation God will bring through it, if we let Him! I made it clear that I liked who I was more so after those experiences than before.

But that wasn't always true!

That often isn't true for many of us. The value systems that have been forced upon us through abuse, deception or manipulation create filters that cause us to "see" lies disguised as truth and lead us into unhealthy choices and changes. Thomas Keating, a Trappist monk, wrote:

> "The instinctual needs that we have when we enter into the world are focused on survival and security, power and control, and affection and esteem. When any of these instinctual needs, which are basically good, are experienced by the child as unfulfilled or withdrawn through abuse and neglect, especially when it is habitual, the child, for survival purposes, may repress those painful, traumatic, emotional experiences in the unconscious. The child may also develop compensatory systems in which he or she tries to find happiness in the gratification of one of those three instinctual needs."[1]

Keating names these systems "programs for happiness" and added that the emotional programs for happiness we develop are attracted to what is acceptable in our culture. And they are almost always unhealthy!

In other words, we were misled and deceived into adjusting our value system in order to satisfy an unfulfilled instinctual need. We bought into a lie! Our tainted filter then created an unhealthy trait or behavior, which impacted ourselves, our spouse and many others in our life. And the reality of that can be overwhelming….

"DID I DO THAT?"

Many of you will recognize that line spoken by the character of Steve Urkel in the 1990s sitcom *Family Matters*. It was usually said not as a question, but after a realization of the consequences resulting from his actions. The last step in becoming intimate with our own self is simply looking at the impact our life has on others.

Seldom do we wake up in the morning and make the decision that we want to harm someone today. But the characteristics we have adopted—and the resulting actions—do inevitably have a great impact on us as well as others, including those we love and, in particular, our spouse.

Self-intimacy requires us to intentionally observe and reflect on the consequences of our behaviors. Sometimes the realization doesn't come until another person points out the impact, as Nathan did to King David (2 Samuel 12), or until years later when there is a revelation of the connection between an action and a result.

Oftentimes the consequences are positive because our behavior is healthy. And for that we should rejoice!

But when we recognize that we have caused harm to another because of our unhealthy choices, there will be a grieving we will experience in the depths of our soul. Know that this pain is actually good and for our benefit because it will lead us to the place of conviction required for refinement.

Each of us has been created by God to be unique—a masterpiece. Although some of our character traits portray His work of art, others, due to our woundedness or unhealthy teaching, mask our beauty. Our self-intimacy work helps us to identify the difference so that the lies can be identified and the truth revealed.

What Is the Truth?

The question is not what is the truth, but rather, *who* is the Truth! God said to Moses in Exodus 3:14, "I am who I am," meaning that God is not defined or determined by anyone or anything other than Himself. If we believe that God is truth, then the filter we must use to determine our identity is Him, through His Word and His Spirit.

Why does it matter?

If we are created in His image, and if our marriage is to reflect His glory, then we—and it—must reflect Him. He does not expect us to be perfect, just transparent and vulnerable, in our relationship with Him—as well as willing to allow Him to transform us so that we can become the epic husband or wife He created us to be.

Knowing who we are and then deciding who we want to be is followed by the question, "How do we get there?" Or in other words, "How do we change?"

Change is a three-step process: awareness, conviction and refinement.

Our *awareness* of who we really are is revealed through self-intimacy as we recognize our real identity; through intimacy with God as He reveals truth to us through His Word and Spirit; and through our relationship with our spouse or another when the person involved has a truth-driven value system and an unselfish desire to see us prosper.

Self-intimacy and a desire for an epic marriage means that constant change is inevitable. Awareness of both our healthy and unhealthy characteristics will come relatively easy.

But simply being aware of something doesn't mean we will move to step two, where we make a life-changing decision. John Maxwell, author and pastor, suggests that we change when we hurt enough that we have to change, or we learn enough that we want to change, or we receive enough that we are able to change.[2]

Awareness moves to *conviction* when we hurt enough, learn enough and receive enough. Conviction requires us to take the critical step of submission, which is giving God permission to do whatever it takes to bring about the third step, refinement. He won't move without it—except to ordain what we need to be convicted.

A telling question that we often ask people when they come in for marriage counseling is, "What are you willing to do (to restore your marriage)?" The only right answer is, "Whatever it takes!" That is submission, which then allows God to bring forth the refinement.

Awareness followed by conviction leads to *refinement*. Malachi 3:3 says that God "will sit as a refiner and purifier of silver...." We don't refine ourselves; we simply participate as we give God permission to change us, and He does the rest. If we are willing to submit to a process of change, why wouldn't we put ourselves into the hands of the One who understands what is needed for us and desires only what is best for us—the One who created us?

We often say that submission to God is simple but not easy. Going through the refinement process is difficult. It usually hurts, it usually lasts too long (in our opinion as we're going through it), and we often can't see the benefits that lie ahead. It's only after going through it a few times and experiencing the joy on the other end do we come to appreciate the process.

There is a story that has circulated on the internet (its original source unknown), that provides a great visual of the concept of God being the great refiner:

> There was a group of women in a Bible study focused on the book of Malachi. When they got to that verse, "He will sit as a refiner and purifier of silver...," they were puzzled, wondering what this statement meant about the character and nature of God.
>
> One of the women offered to find out about the process of refining silver and get back to the group at their next Bible study. That week this woman called up a silversmith and made an appointment to watch him at work. She didn't mention anything about the reason for her interest in silver beyond her curiosity about the process of refining silver. As she watched the silversmith, he held a piece of silver over the fire and let it heat up. He explained that in refining silver, one needed to hold the silver in the middle of the fire where the flames were hottest to burn away all the impurities. The woman thought about God holding us in such a hot spot as the refiner and purifier of silver.
>
> She asked the silversmith if it was true that he had to sit there in front of the fire the whole time the silver was being refined. The man answered that yes, he not only had to sit there holding the silver, but he also had to keep his eyes on the silver the entire time it was in the fire. If the silver was left even a moment too long in the flames, it would be destroyed. The woman was silent for a moment. Then she asked the silversmith, "How do you know when the silver is fully refined?"
>
> He smiled at her and answered, "Oh, that's easy—when I see my image in it."

Refinement is not easy. It works best only when the flame is the hottest so that all of the "impurities" are burned away. That's painful. But we need to always remember that God is watching and in control the whole time, never taking us off the fire too soon or leaving us on it too long. We also must keep in mind and look forward to the purpose of the refinement: to look like Him!

Our minds inform our affections of what will bring us the greatest happiness; our affections create a desire for it; and our will chooses to pursue it. When our greatest happiness comes from anywhere or anything other than God, our actions will lead to disappointment for ourselves and others.

Plus, it is a guarantee that we are not the same today as we were yesterday, and we will not be the same tomorrow as we are today. The question is, is the change for good? And what part do we play in that process?

Self-intimacy brings awareness. A desire to change brings conviction. And when we give God permission to do whatever is needed, He refines us.

Intimacy with one's own self helps each of us understand who we are.

Intimacy with God, the topic of the next chapter, helps us understand who we were created to be.

REFLECTION

At the end of the previous chapter, you identified some of your unhealthy behaviors. Now that you know what they are, consider the following:

- How do you feel when you are doing them?
- How do they impact those around you?
- Are you convicted to give God permission to do whatever it takes to refine you?
- If not, what is holding you back?

Pick some healthy behaviors and do the same exercise.

CHAPTER 7

INTIMACY WITH GOD

WE WERE IN THE PROCESS OF BUILDING a new house and needed a place to rent during the transition. Some friends had a coach house on their property that provided a comfortable space for the few months we would need it. It was a large piece of property, and the coach house was towards the back, well off of the road and away from any city lights.

Early one winter morning, I (Mike) walked out the door and was immediately overcome by the vastness and the brightness of the stars. It was one of those moments when your soul is deeply aware of God's glory in His creation. I just stood there for a few minutes taking it all in and praising the One who created that moment for me.

But the best part was yet to come!

I finally broke away from the moment of awe and climbed into my car. When I turned the key to start the car, there was that momentary silence before the radio kicks on. Then the silence was broken by these six words, sung out of the radio: "Our God is an awesome God...."

Tears began to roll down my cheeks as I recognized the miracle of God's timing in that moment. Had I waited a few seconds longer or started the car a few seconds earlier; had the radio been turned off or tuned to a different station; or had the radio station picked a different song to play at that time…the moment would have ended with "just" me being in awe of our Creator.

But God ordained that moment for me! For Him and me! And when I realized He had created a miracle for just my benefit, the tears turned to joyful weeping. Even with all that He had to attend to in those few moments, He authored an intimate moment that He chose to share with me alone!

THE CIRCLE OF PURSUIT

Intimacy: A Relationship of Deep, Genuine Affection

It makes sense that we can choose to have an intimacy with our own self. It kind of makes sense that we can have intimacy with another person (that is, when the other person chooses to participate as well). But to have intimacy with God?

Yet, we can! Hallelujah!

We stated earlier that God's design for marriage cannot exist without intimacy: two "shall become one" (Genesis 2:24). We went a step further to say that in order to be intimate with our spouse, we first need to know ourselves so that, as our transparent and vulnerable self, we can step into the intimate relationship with God that was waiting for us when God chose to create us. We also pointed out that self-intimacy precedes intimacy with God, which precedes intimacy with others—not due to importance, but to progression.

Clearly, intimacy with God is the foundation of our existence.

The Bible is filled with great stories of intimacy between God (as Father, Son and Holy Spirit) and one of His children. One of the most inspiring stories is in Exodus where we read about the relationship between God and Moses. The Israelites are a few years into their desert journey to the Promised Land when they reject God in favor of an idol: a golden calf. The interaction between God and Moses reveals the genuineness of their relationship as God shares His anger with Moses, and Moses pleads with God to fulfill His covenant with His people.

There is a tremendous amount of revelation to unpack in this story, but the two moments we want to highlight speak greatly of the intimate relationship that we can—and should—have with God. The first is in the statement that the Lord spoke "to Moses face to face, as a man speaks to his friend" (Exodus 33:11). Imagine having a conversation with Jesus with His forehead touching yours!

The second (also in Exodus 33) is when God tells Moses that he can go ahead and lead the people on to the Promised Land, their dream destination, the land flowing with milk and honey—but with the caveat that He was not going with them. Moses then reveals his greatest desire—his intimacy with God—as he declares he would rather stay in the desert than be in the Promised Land without Him.

Forty-five years ago, we both stepped out of operating in a religious relationship with our Lord and began to desire one of intimacy. The difference has been and continues to become more and more astounding, since we still have a long way to go. The journey has been one of *continually submitting to God's pursuit of us* and *choosing to continually pursue Him*, of seeking to better know God and allowing Him to better know us.

Having said that, we think it is important to add a two-part disclaimer before you move forward in this chapter. The first is a reiteration of a previous comment: The purpose of self-intimacy is to just be authentic in your relationship with God, even while still very unrefined. It's a "come as we are" pursuit, trusting that He will refine us to become who He created us to be. And second, it is a journey to a destination that we never fully reach (because we grow in knowledge and understanding of God through eternity).

We hope to provide a bit of encouragement for the next step of the journey toward greater intimacy with God and the relief that it happens one step at a time. Scripture says that we grow from one revelation to the next (2 Corinthians 3:18). It comes intentionally from God, piece by piece, as He chooses and as we are able to receive Him.

Submit to His Pursuit

We have played countless games of hide-and-seek with our grandkids. It was very interesting to watch them gain understanding of the purpose of the game as they became older. Initially, there was a great desire on their part to be found. They didn't want to be "lost" for a second but loved that we were trying to "find" them. As they grew in wisdom, they quickly learned that to win the game meant that you stayed "lost."

Is that an analogy of our intimacy journey with God?

Our initial connection with our Lord is one of great excitement. We love that He continually pursues us, like a shepherd looking for the one lost sheep (Luke 15:4–7), and that He always has (Psalm 139:13)! We love that He knows everything about us (Psalm 139:4), and that He wants to dwell with us forever (Revelation 21:3)! It is a very emotionally driven relationship in the beginning, much like it was with the two of us when we first started dating.

But then we grow in maturity, and we think we know God and how He looks upon us. In our transparency with ourselves, and per-haps through faulty teaching, we choose to hide, and we doubt that God would want to spend time seeking us. Isn't that what Adam and Eve did (Genesis 3)? God came to walk in the garden with them, but because they had been deceived (taught that they shouldn't trust in God) and realized they were naked (self-intimacy), they hid. They could have walked in the garden with the One who created them, *but they hid*!

None of our grandkids are missing. The hide-and-seek games never end with anyone not found. Why? At the end of the day, our greatest desire is to be in each other's presence—like God's desire with us. And so, He made a way because He doesn't want to be with-out us for a moment, for forever!

It's interesting that our family has moved on to a different vari-ation of hide-and-seek to a game popularly known as "Sardines." In this game, one person hides and the rest try to find him or her. When they do, they squeeze into the hiding place with the original hider. In hide-and-seek, if the "seekers" give up, those hiding will be lost forever. In Sardines, the game ends when all are together.

Our intimacy with God is certainly not a game. Yet don't we often make it into one by trying to hide from the One who wants to just be with us? Our faith journey is a constant growing in knowledge and understanding of God, of seeking Him. It is also a constant submit-ting to His pursuit of us so that we may be "found"!

For God, the purpose is fulfilled when we are all together, all found. And at that moment, the "game" doesn't end but rather begins!

If there was a specific process to follow to submit to God's pursuit of us, we would certainly share it with you. What we know to be true is that the greater our revelation knowledge of God (knowledge revealed directly to our heart by the Spirit of God), the easier it is to submit. It is in our pursuit of intimacy with Him that our desire to be "found" increases.

Here is one more disclaimer: God is more concerned with our heart than our accomplishments. Although intimacy should be our focus, it must come from desire and not fear. When our girls were small, my (Diane's) time was not always mine to control. Someone suggested I take five minutes to journal every day. Although that was a desire, it was often not possible—and it caused me to feel guilty. But I quickly realized that God knew the season I was in and that I would have loved to spend that dedicated time with Him. Instead, He was with me as I changed diapers, read books and took walks. He pursued me in my season of life and found me in the "place" I needed to be!

Pursuing Intimacy with God

In the movie *Date Night*, the husband and wife play this game where they present a "story" about another couple dining in the same restaurant they are. The story they share is totally based upon what they see and hear and has no bearing on what is factual. They don't *know* the other couple.

Don't we often do the same when it comes to Jesus? We live our life based on what we have "seen" and "heard" regarding our Lord, and yet we do not really know Him! The only difference between the couple in the movie and us is that they know that they don't know the truth. We usually believe that we do.

We will often ask people to describe the God that they don't believe in (yes, it's a trick question). When they do, we will often respond that we wouldn't believe in that god either, followed by a great sadness if they don't desire to learn the truth about Jesus!

That is our journey: seeking the truth by pursuing intimacy with God.

We both grew up believing that we had to earn God's love. Our picture of Him was that He was punishing, controlling and, most often, absent. That was our truth—until we received the revelation knowledge that we had been believing a lie. Initially, a major part of our pursuit of intimacy was recognizing and admitting that we had been deceived and that we had to renounce a number of lies, forgive those who taught us those lies, forgive ourselves for believing them, and ask God to reveal His truth.

Diane's Story

I have always been a very disciplined person. Even as I child, I learned to create routines that gave me control, like always "saying my prayers" before I went to bed. I would have said that I truly believed God was going to answer my prayers, but at the same time I would experience fear if I hadn't "followed" my religious disciplines. My control created anxiety because I had to *do* all the right things to be in good relationship with God.

At the faith renewal weekend we talked about earlier, there was a song that I resonated with, about being *friends* with Jesus, which was a new concept for me. Knowing that true friendship wasn't about control and doing, it radically changed my relationship with Him. I wanted the intimacy that Moses experienced when God talked to him as a friend. I wanted Jesus to no longer consider me a slave but a friend, like He proclaimed to His disciples at the Last Supper.

I wanted to pursue intimacy with God, not out of control, but out of submission—out of freedom.

And somehow, I knew that I first had a lot to learn about myself.

Intimacy with myself and intimacy with God…both have been, and still are, a journey.

HOW?

Once again, it is simple—but not easy.

It seems popular to teach a specific, linear approach to submitting to God's pursuit of us and our pursuit of Him. That's what we experienced early on. We had to dispel a lot of shame because we weren't doing it "right" and weren't checking all of the required boxes. The "aha" moment came when we heard someone state the obvious: "Why would an infinite God create a finite path to intimacy with Him?" He wouldn't, and because He created each of us to have unique preferences in our value system, we should be somewhat unique in our connection with the One who created us to be unique.

Still, there are some basics that add value in our pursuit of intimacy with God.

The obvious are *reading scripture* and *prayer*. What's not so obvious is the structure of that. The two of us have read the Bible cover to cover, through a daily one-year program, as a part of an in-depth study on a particular book, topically, as part of daily devotional references, using different translations and (one of our favorites) as part of a two-year study of the life of Jesus taught by a Messianic Jewish organization. All of these programs and methods have been fruitful simply because we're reading the Word. But sometimes they've been a chore—like the second time I (Mike) started to read the Bible in one year or started reading the Psalms in a particular translation. Fortunately, we have learned to read scripture as a desire and not a box to check.

Our prayer life has been a journey of its own as we have moved into greater and greater intimacy with our Lord. Our posture has changed from doing most of the talking to mostly listening through the Holy Spirit and seeking His will as opposed to convincing Him to bless us with what we want. As we have stepped into a prayer life of communion, we have realized the power available to us through prayer!

Having a mentor/spiritual director helps us to create and maintain a healthy pursuit of God. Working with counselors has helped us to heal from our trauma and eliminate the barriers we have put up that keep us from receiving His love. Processing life with like-minded people allows the giving and receiving of encouragement and validation. Seeing Him in nature and praising Him in song opens our hearts to the joy of knowing Him and being known by Him. And on and on....

The point is *to connect*!

We shared earlier that we both have our space to spend dedicated time with God each morning. It usually ends up being at the same time due to our sleep patterns. We often are even reading the same daily devotional at the same time. But even though our time with God has many similarities, our connection with Him is still unique because we are unique. And we have great spiritual intimacy with each other because we are often sharing our dedicated connecting time revelations with each other.

Our best advice may simply be to do it. If it isn't drawing you closer to God, change it. But keep seeking Him!

Mike's Story
Almost by accident, I created a format that I have used consistently every day in my dedicated connecting time with God for the past five or six years. Not to brag, but I haven't missed a single day because I desire it. I need it.

That wasn't always the case. I wanted to be that guy who said, "Good morning, Lord," before I got out of bed. I wanted to be that guy who looked forward to opening my Bible rather than feeling I had to. I wanted to be that guy who heard and responded to God's voice and wrote down His thoughts in my journal. I wanted to be that guy…but I wasn't. At least not consistently.

That all changed through a 90-day period of disciplined eating for the purpose of getting healthy physically. That was great in itself as I changed my lifestyle relative to food. But at the same time, I decided to also be disciplined spiritually. As a result, I became much more like "that guy" I had wanted to be all along.

That connecting time did start off as a designated period of checking boxes: studying His Word, listening, journaling and, most of all, expressing my gratitude. But that discipline quickly morphed into desire. Then that desire led to greater intimacy, and it continues to do so each day. I have been able to share that format with a number of other men with the caveat that they tweak it to make it their own. Their feedback has been very positive. Their period of discipline has also turned to desire, which has led to greater intimacy.

This chapter could go on and on sharing thoughts and wisdom on the benefits of submitting to God's pursuit of us and our pursuit of intimacy with Him. Trust us when we say that if you make it a priority, He will ordain it. And you will benefit greatly!

We celebrated Diane's birthday not long ago with the 11 of us. Each of the five grandkids shared why they loved Doddie (her special name to them). Each one brought tears to our eyes—even the two and a half year old. But perhaps the words that caused us all to say "wow" and "amen" were these: "Because she loves me!"

We love Him (and each other) because He first loved us (1 John 4:19)! We desire to be intimate with Him (and each other) because He first desired to be intimate with us! We pursue intimacy with Him because He pursues intimacy with us. And we achieve intimacy with Him because He always knows where we're hiding and that our true desire is to be found!

Hallelujah!

REFLECTION

Can you think of a time when you played hide-and-seek with God?
- Do you know why/what you were/are hiding?
- Who won?
  (Aren't you glad He did?)
- Do you find yourself playing hide-and-seek with your spouse?
  (Does anybody win in that game?)

PART 3

INTIMACY—OUR PART

CHAPTER 8

COVENANT AS ONE

ACKNOWLEDGING WHO WE ARE (INTIMACY WITH OUR own self); determining who we want to be (*intimacy with God*); and the results of the three-step change process (*awareness, conviction, refinement*), will prepare us to be the complete person it is necessary for us to be so that "*two shall become one*."

A few years ago, we celebrated our 40th wedding anniversary with a weekend away at a resort in Wisconsin. Saturday afternoon we were relaxing on the balcony overlooking the vast courtyard that led down to the lake. It was a beautiful, sunny June day—perfect for the wedding that was to take place below us.

Everything was upbeat and positive as the procession began, and it ended with the bride being escorted down the aisle by her father. She took her place next to the groom, and the two of them held hands as the pastor began the ceremony. He looked at the groom and said these words: "Jonathan, I want you to know that Laurie is *not* the *one* for you." There may have been an audible gasp as the guests heard the words, and, most definitely, there was a look of horror on the faces of the bride and groom.

Then the pastor looked at the bride and said, "And Laurie, I want you to know that Jonathan is *not* the *one* for you." At this point, the guests were wondering who was going to grab this guy and end this travesty!

Then the pastor said something brilliant! "…Until you say '*I do.*' And then, Jonathan, Laurie is *the one for you*, and, Laurie, Jonathan is *the one for you!*"

We have talked about intimacy with our own self and intimacy with God. We have stressed the importance of creating that connection prior to stepping into intimacy with another person in marriage. *In fact, we can't stress that enough!* We hope and pray that that process has begun and will be ongoing for you, especially as we move forward into understanding intimacy with our spouse.

GOD PROCLAIMS OUR ONENESS

When God created marriage, He *declared* that the two (husband and wife) shall become *one*! Jesus affirmed that as He again *declared* that the "two shall become one flesh" as recorded in Matthew and Mark's Gospels. We've emphasized the word *declare* because of the importance of how God creates—He creates with His voice. He *spoke* the world and all that is in it into creation!

We have done some research and heard some amazing teaching on the power of the frequency of sound. Pour some sand on a metal plate attached to the top of an audio speaker and watch how it is formed into different shapes as the frequency changes. It's fascinating to watch. In the same way, the body responds differently to different frequencies. From healing, to learning, to producing, we respond differently if there is music of a certain frequency playing in the room. That makes sense! If God created with His voice, shouldn't we respond differently to different sounds?

We propose that God spoke marriage into creation as well, and that in order for our marriage to be epic (as He intended), we must resonate with the "frequency" of what He created: *oneness!* That is a relationship where your spouse is *the one* for you, lived out through the covenantal design.

In Chapter 2, we talked about God's design of marriage as a covenant. As a quick reminder, there are three parts: 1) each of you vows to God that you agree that His plan is best and you will commit to follow it; 2) each of you vows to the other that you will fulfill His plan with that specific person; and 3) God vows with the two of you as one that you will now enter into His promise of great joy within this properly beautiful thing called marriage.

The question you reflected on at the end of Chapter 2 was whether you entered into a contract or covenant on your wedding day. If it was a contract, it is not too late; it is imperative that your marriage from this day forward become a covenant relationship with each other and with God.

I'm not sure at what point we could fully say our marriage was that of a covenant. We both had full intentions of each other being the "one" when we said "I do." But were we really capable of that at that point in our relationship with ourselves and with God? Regardless, today we are capable! And we are one!

On June 9, 2024, we celebrated our 45th wedding anniversary at a little Italian restaurant, watching the sunset over the water, with food, drink and conversation. Diane had captured a list of life events that we had experienced during our marriage, and it was a tremendous time of intimacy as we reflected on those moments of "for better" and "for worse."

We have *so* many memories to be grateful for over our years together that the list would go on for pages. Likely we would be forgetting as many as we remembered. But what was interesting to discover in our reflection that evening was that for many of the "for better" moments, there was a similar "for worse" moment.

We spent lots of time and energy designing and building a house together—only to experience a major fire and watch it burn.

We started and changed careers together—and walked away from careers that didn't work out.

We welcomed two beautiful daughters into this world and helped them to become amazing women who are raising up delightful children of their own. And we experienced the horrible tragedy of losing a son without the joy of raising him.

For better and for worse—we are grateful for both, for God was and is always with us, and we were and are one with Him and with each other in all of them! Because through them, we have learned to give God permission to refine us. Through them, we have chosen to seek greater intimacy with our own self, with Him and with each other. And He has fulfilled His promise to refine us for His glory and our benefit.

As naïve as we might have been on our wedding day, we have continually pressed into the oneness God created and declared over us when we said, "I do." As we shared earlier, our desire for oneness became our priority when we chose to pursue an epic marriage. Oneness with our spouse is nothing more than a choice (that is, a conviction) on our part to let the One who created us and created marriage do what He does best: refine us so that we reflect His image and so that our marriage does, too!

Remember that God's refinement only comes when we are convicted to give Him permission to do so. Our awareness moves to conviction when we hurt enough that we have to change or when we learn enough that we want to change or when we receive enough that we are able to change. Here's a gem of wisdom we learned through the change process: operating in the "learn enough" category is a lot less painful and takes a lot less time!

Our Story
We had to learn the hard way.

Losing our son Ryan was—and is—a life-changing experience. Even though we were surrounded by love and support, the grief was overwhelming. Day after day, we wondered how we would survive. To this day it is a wonder to us that we did, and that our intimacy with our own self, with God and with each other were strengthened as a result. That's the beauty of choosing to pursue intimacy! Even in the hardest of times, there is joy in the revelations we experience.

Initially, there were periods of unhealthy behavior as we struggled with our grief—moments that threatened to tear us apart. We didn't know any better, so this became one of those times when we had to get to the place of "hurting enough" before we gave God permission to do whatever He needed to do in order to refine us. What could have destroyed our marriage ended up being what God used to turn us toward oneness with Him and each other.

One of the greatest moments of intimacy we have experienced together was the morning we received the phone call that our first grandchild was born—a boy! We just held on to each other, weeping in celebration with the joy of that moment, for our kids and for us! But there was something more. In that moment we renounced the lie (the fear) that, in our family, we don't get to bring little boys home from the hospital. And we took another step of healing, *together*!

It is not fun to experience those "hurt enough" moments that cause us to have to change, especially when we can experience those "learn enough" moments when we want and choose to change. We experienced the result of one of those not too long ago.

I (Mike) had a hip replaced. One of the core values that is prevalent in our immediate family is the correlation and importance of body, mind and spirit. We spend a lot of time and effort improving and maintaining each part, and we continually seek God's refinement—including in our frustration when we're struggling physically. In December of 2024, we had another significant moment of oneness that was birthed out of a difficult time.

For years, we both had struggled with limitations caused by illness or injury—even to the point of denying, perhaps isolating and definitely creating an environment that would cause the other to want to pull away. We never did, but it often wasn't pretty.

Fortunately, we recognized the unhealthiness of our behaviors and sought to change them because of the impact they had on the other and our marriage during those seasons. Before we got to that "hurt enough" place, we chose to be honest with ourselves and to be vulnerable with God, giving Him permission to refine us. He did.

At one point, a couple of weeks into rehab, we had a moment where we shared with each other the intimacy that had been created as I (Mike) let Diane take care of me with great appreciation, and the great joy Diane received in serving my needs as I recovered.

God's declaration of oneness was again evident in His refinement.

Whether we hurt enough or learn enough, the key is still God's refinement. The change in us and in our marriage doesn't last when we try to do it without Him. One of the consistent themes we see in couples who move toward an epic marriage is that they have created an environment that allows them to "receive enough" that they are able to change. In other words, they maintain a safe environment that is built on a solid foundation of trust in God and each other.

ASSUME WITH GRACE

How often do we operate out of assumptions? How often do we jump to conclusions based on those assumptions, even when what we are assuming is contrary to what we have experienced in the past? One of the great benefits of intimacy in marriage is growing in understanding of our spouse's heart and value system. How often does our spouse do or say something that doesn't reflect his or her true nature—a comment or action based out of defensiveness or because of an old wound? We assume he or she is intentionally trying to hurt us.

What if, instead, we gave our spouse the benefit of the doubt? What if we assumed that we misunderstood or that he or she was struggling for some reason?

What if, instead, we asked a question before we responded? What if we asked for clarification of what was said and meant rather than reacting out of assumed hurt?

What if we asked if he or she is okay because those actions or words didn't reflect our spouse's true nature?

What if we focused on our spouse rather than ourselves?

Again, it's a choice. If we are operating in covenant, we will choose to love unconditionally rather than responsively.

One of the constant teachings of marriage ministries is to regularly have date nights. That is a great idea because it provides a method of enhancing social intimacy—an evening of time to laugh, relax and have fun together.

We also suggest that couples include regular "conversation dates" into their relationship routine—to intentionally and regularly set aside a time and place where each spouse can safely ask (and answer) the simple questions: "What did I do that blessed you this week?" "What did I do that created difficulty for you?" The only rules are to be good listeners and not get defensive, only asking questions for clarity.

Shouldn't we desire to know what blesses our spouse so that we can continue doing it? And shouldn't we want to know what causes difficulty for our spouse so that we can stop and change? It is so encouraging when we realize our spouse is interested in loving well!

It's also a good opportunity to learn more about each other. Find a book of questions written for couples that is geared toward greater understanding, with questions like, "What was your most embarrassing moment in high school?" or "What was a life-defining moment growing up?" or "When did you laugh so hard that your drink came out of your nose?" Even after more than 45 years together, there are still things we are learning about each other.

Create an environment that allows each other and your marriage to reflect and grow so that it better reflects God's glory.

Oneness with God and each other is a choice. Refinement is not pleasant—until it's done. And it is never completely done. But there are moments along the way when we just need to pause, recognize and celebrate the joy that has resulted from our choice to let God refine us and refine our marriage.

Acknowledging who we are (*intimacy with our own self*); determining who we want to be (*intimacy with God*); and the results of the three-step change process (*awareness, conviction, refinement*) will prepare us to be the complete person it is necessary for us to be so that "*two shall become one.*"

A properly beautiful marriage is a choice: one that is available to every couple who chooses to follow God's design for marriage. Its foundation is intimacy.

In the chapters ahead, we will explore what God's design might look like as part of the different types of intimacy we should be experiencing in our marriage relationship.

REFLECTION

Husbands, plan a "conversation date" with your wife. Here are your guidelines:

- Find a time and place that is safe, comfortable and allows for uninterrupted conversation.

- Ask each other the two basic questions:
    "What was great this past week?"
    "What was difficult this past week?"
- Come up with two other fun questions that you have never asked each other before.
- *Listen* and enjoy each other's answers.
- Before you leave, each of you ask and answer this final question:
    "Do you choose to pursue an epic marriage?"

CHAPTER 9

WHAT'S IN THE WAY?

THERE IS AN OLDER COUPLE IN OUR community whom we often see taking walks together. Seldom are they not holding hands as they walk—a display of intimacy. It reminds us of the beautiful visual of Adam and Eve walking together in the Garden. What enhances that image of the first man and woman is that God was walking with them.

Until they hid!

Scripture says that Adam and Eve physically hid from God. But they also, in a way, hid from each other. They realized that they were naked, and they *covered themselves*. To this day, there is an ongoing struggle for husbands and wives to be vulnerable and transparent. The lies put forth by the evil one created destruction where God intended good. This destruction is probably no more apparent than in the way the world has recreated God's beautiful design of marriage.

When the man and the woman accepted the lie of Satan, they stepped out of the covenant of oneness that God had proclaimed over marriage. God revealed the battle that husbands and wives would now experience as a result: "To the woman he said, '...Your desire shall be contrary to your husband, but he shall rule over you'" (Genesis 3:16).

Motivational speaker Jeff VanVonderen puts it this way: "God simply revealed the self-centered core that began to motivate each of them: the woman would continue to try to draw life and nurturing from a man who was not capable of filling these deep needs—never was and never will be. And the man would be forever trying to rule over the woman, either aggressively or passively trying to keep her quiet about his inadequacy to fill her needs."[1]

Some days it may feel like there is a curse on your marriage, *but* it doesn't have to be that way! Maybe all it takes is a filter change.

"If it's not good for your marriage, it's not good for either one of you!" Our spiritual mentor spoke those words to the congregation one morning, and we have adopted that statement as the filter that should be used for every couple seeking to live out an epic marriage.

There is a great book entitled *With* by Skye Jethani that challenges readers to explore the way in which they live out their relationship with God. Four popular, but false, ways are: life from God, life over God, life for God and life under God. The truth is that we should be living out a relationship *with* God.

This challenge is also relevant in our marriage relationship.

If we choose to live our relationship with our spouse in a way that seeks our value and happiness *from* the other person, we set ourselves—and our spouse—up for failure. Upon reflecting back to the curse, it is *not* God's design that our identity should come from anything or anyone but the One who created us. We will be disappointed because our spouse is not capable of providing that value and because joy only comes from God. (Remember His part of the covenant?)

Life *over* our spouse is very similar in that we have an expectation of what our spouse should do for us. It is the epitome of a contract marriage. Even as a couple tries to follow marriage models, implement tools for a good marriage, or seek counsel, the focus isn't on what is best for the marriage, but rather it is on "what do I want," or more desperately, on "what do I need?"

Life from and over our spouse is clearly from selfish desires in that each spouse is focused on getting what he or she wants or needs. Living life *for* or *under* our spouse, on the surface, seems much more focused on loving sacrificially rather than selfishly. But if we dig a little deeper, our real motivation will be discovered in that our pur-pose is not about intimacy with each other; rather, it is about show-casing an "obedient heart." In other words, we are trying to glorify ourselves rather than glorify God's perfect design for marriage.

Living a life *for* our spouse can take on a number of appearances, none of which are genuine. Many of them don't reflect what goes on when others are not around to "see it." Yes, we want others to see God reflected in our marriage, but that should be a result of liv-ing out our covenant and not an agenda. We have done premarital counseling with a number of couples where there was much stress around the wedding ceremony because they wanted to make sure they would represent God well. Their ceremony lacked joy because they were focused on "doing" it the right way instead of celebrating the covenant God had created for them to step into. Their marriages continued along the same lines until they came back for counseling to find a new direction.

In the same way, a marriage focused on life *under* our spouse is not genuine either. It is focused on obedience and not choice. We see marriage after marriage that lacks joy and only exists because the couple wants to be obedient to their wedding vows. They don't want to miss God's blessing by ending their relationship. But that becomes their only focus. They have forgotten the part about oneness. Yes, God hates divorce, but He is also grieved over a marriage that doesn't reveal the beauty of intimacy with Him and each other.

How do you know if your marriage is focused on a life from, over, for or under your spouse? Again, that's where self-intimacy comes into play, along with an understanding of our motivation. When we live out of a false posture in how we relate to God or to our spouse, our motivation is most likely based on fear rather than on desire. Fear motivates us to do what we have to do in order to calm ourselves, avoid conflict or get our way. We are afraid of the consequences if we don't satisfy our spouse's "needs," and it usually involves manipulation.

Desire, however, is focused on honoring and serving our spouse. It will move us into what God created: a relationship lived out *with* our spouse. Just like we are created to live a relationship *with* God, we are also created to live a relationship *with* our spouse.

That will be a natural result if we focus on His design and seek the intimacy He created it to contain. Then our purpose of glorifying Him will be fulfilled!

The idea of living in a relationship with each other also maintains the focus of "marriage first." We enter marriage as two individuals and work to become "one flesh." When our life is filtered through "what's best for our marriage," we are trusting God's design and His promise that joy will overflow as a result.

One point of clarification: by becoming "one flesh," we are *not* giving up our individual identities; rather, we are combining them into a relationship that is unique because of the two individuals involved. I (Diane) am a wife, mother, counselor, friend, etc. That is my identity, which is lived out fully within my marriage to Mike. I (Mike) also have many roles that are lived out within our marriage. The same holds true for our daughters and their husbands as they seek an epic marriage. But while all of our marriages will have the same foundation, each will be unique—its own masterpiece and not a reproduction.

A perfectly beautiful marriage is a unique masterpiece that lies on top of the masterpiece that each of us is.

WHAT GETS IN THE WAY?

In the Introduction, we discussed the role that complacency had played in keeping our marriage from moving toward epic. Good became the enemy of great. Had we not made this discovery and then chose to pursue an epic marriage, it's very possible we would still be married today, just missing out on the intimacy with our own self, with God and with each other that has resulted in great joy.

Every marriage hits a speed bump or a detour at some point, and for many reasons. Some overcome the obstacle, and their marriage ends up stronger than before. Some suppress it, and their marriage continues as a relationship between two roommates (who usually don't get along). Others quickly give up hope and file for divorce.

Interestingly, if we ask a group of couples what they believe the main reasons for divorce are, they will quickly name incompatibility (that is, a difference in values), finances, sex (lack of intimacy or infidelity), and communication problems as the top answers.

An October 2024 Forbes article on divorce confirms that they are not far off. What is even more interesting is that the article also revealed the top reasons couples married in the first place—and found that there was a high correlation between those and the reasons they cited for choosing divorce.[2] A recent conversation we had with a couple revealed that their rush to get married was so that they wouldn't have sex outside of marriage. Ten years later, they are having physical intimacy issues.

In other words, most marriages fail because the individuals have the wrong motivation to start with. Their marriage is a contract and ends up being broken.

In our years of working with couples, we have witnessed this truth firsthand:

Contract marriage is the leading cause of divorce!

On the other hand, a covenant relationship usually withstands the trials that are common in most marriages. When the couple encounters a conflict, they partner with God and each other to overcome it (this process is discussed in greater detail in Chapter 12). Financial difficulties, intimacy issues, communication problems, value differences, etc., are opportunities to strengthen the relationship, not destroy it—*unless* the reasons lead to a spirit of *bitterness*.

If our expectations of each other are not met, we feel hurt or disrespected. "He doesn't tell me I'm pretty." "She doesn't greet me at the door when I come home." If left unattended, that hurt can lead to bitterness, even in a covenantal relationship. When asked what led to their marriage's demise, most couples can't remember a specific event. But because the hurt was never addressed and effectively resolved, bitterness takes hold and grows into what seems like an insurmountable reality.

At one of our marriage workshops, a couple that had had a very difficult experience getting through the session the previous evening was notably absent the following morning. It was assumed that they were done with both the workshop and their marriage. (It was that bad!) We were all surprised when they walked in almost two hours late. We were even more surprised that there was joy and hope on their faces and in what they shared.

They still had a lot of issues they needed to work through, but they had eliminated the spirit of bitterness that had crept into their relationship. (The exercise they used is included as Appendix A.)

Bitterness Is Evil

The apostle Paul makes it very clear in his letter to the Ephesians that "we do not wrestle against flesh and blood, but against the…spiritual forces of evil…" (6:12). There are many names used to describe the devil in the Bible, such as Satan or the evil one. But it's Jesus who labels him as *the enemy* because it is the purpose of Satan and his army of evil to turn us away from God and from good—*and therefore from epic marriage.*

Through lies and deception, evil creates chaos in our relationship with our spouse and we end up with not two becoming one, but one opposed to the other. A favorite verse shared at wedding ceremonies is Ecclesiastes 4:12: "And though a man might prevail against one who is alone, two will withstand him—a threefold cord is not quickly broken." But if evil turns us against each other, we stand a good chance of falling (and of our marriage failing). However, if we stand together with our spouse and the Holy Spirit against the darkness this world throws at us, good will prevail.

Our recommendation is that it is extremely valuable to gain freedom from the evil of bitterness before focusing on the specific obstacles that surface in your marriage. Again, Appendix A is a resource for you to use to gain this freedom, along with counseling and/or spiritual direction.

WE ARE DIFFERENT PER DESIGN

In addition to eliminating bitterness, another precursor to effective conflict resolution (see Chapter 12) is understanding our created differences. We are created by design—created by God!

We can read the creation story in Genesis 1 and 2, how God (Father, Son and Spirit) created the heavens and the earth. He separated the light from the darkness, the water from the dry land, and the day from the night. Each part of His creation was necessary and distinct. And He proclaimed that all that He had made was good.

Then He made man! In His image! To reflect His glory! With responsibility to manage all that He had created. And He separated His creation into male and female, each separate and distinct. Then, seeing His image reflected in the man and the woman, He proclaimed that it was very good!

Before we go any further, we need to make this statement: "Separate and distinct" does *not* mean that there is a distinction in value! As we discuss differences between a man and a woman, we are not dismissing the uniqueness that is part of each of us—uniqueness that is sometimes natural and sometimes learned.

We previously introduced the idea that men and women approach intimacy differently and that it is helpful to understand both our own and our spouse's uniqueness. As we look at living out our intimacy as part of our marriage, those differences are worth exploring in greater detail.

Much research has been done and many books have been written about the differences between a man and a woman. That we are different physically has been obvious since our creation, as strength, appearance and genitalia are easily observable. The idea that our brains are also different has been a more recent discovery. The idea that it is a result of creation rather than culture has been scientifically accepted as well. Thoughts and behaviors that are common across different cultures when there had never been any cross-cultural interaction display God's original design in His creation of man distinct from woman.

WE. ARE. DIFFERENT. FOR. A. REASON.

Those differences need to be validated and celebrated—with discernment as to which differences are natural versus which are learned.

Here's an example. Through surveys conducted by author Shaunti Feldhahn, the vast majority of women (79%) operate as if there are multiple windows open on their computer screen and they are constantly and rapidly moving their attention back and forth between

85

tasks so that none of them are neglected.[3] If the same research was done with men, it is likely that an even greater percentage would say they operate with only one window open at a time. They will likely close that one window before they open another one. Research of male and female brains would indicate there is a difference in our wiring as the reason.

When we recognize that fact, it helps us create a system in our relationship that fosters partnership rather than separation in our day-to-day connection. If I (Mike) am watching The Masters (golf tournament) and Diane asks me a question without first getting my attention, she likely will think I am ignoring her. Pausing the telecast (in other words, closing the window) will allow me to "open" the window related to her question.

On the other hand, if I (Diane) am trying to enjoy a relaxing din-ner with Mike, it helps if I can shut down (that is, resolve) as many windows as possible so that the "us" window gets the primary focus. It is even possible that Mike can help me close those windows if he is aware of what they are.

We understand our created differences and have turned frustra-tion into connection.

Just as it is important to appreciate our value system differences (the ones that don't deal with basic morals), it is also important to appreciate our created differences. What we have learned from our efforts is that it is extremely helpful (and fun) in our intimacy work to do so. Learning how God made us draws us into greater intimacy with our own self and with Him. Learning about our spouse does the same with each other.

Our purpose here is not to provide you with a vast amount of knowledge on our created differences; rather, it is to make you aware that it is important (and fun) to understand and encourage you to seek it out. There are a number of books and articles that provide researched information on this topic.

We will add some more discoveries in future chapters, but here are a couple of thoughts to consider:

What a man most wishes his wife knew about him: *How much I love her!*

What a woman most wishes her husband knew about her:
I do deeply need, respect and desire him!

How different would your relationship be if you believed that?

BROKEN TOGETHER

There's an often used saying attributed to philosopher Friedrich Nietzsche that what doesn't kill you makes you stronger. As we experience obstacles in our marriage, we learn that what doesn't result in divorce can lead to an epic marriage. But, although Nietzsche ignored God's role in our healing, our marriage transformation cannot! Yes, many Christ-centered marriages incur trauma that the couple cannot overcome. But couples that are not one with Him will never attain the intimacy that is available according to God's promise!

The group Casting Crowns has a song entitled "Broken Together" that will bring to tears any couple who has survived the obstacles their marriage has faced. By the grace of God, we have experienced the result of our marriage becoming stronger as a result of walking through trials *together*!

It bears repeating that God designed marriage to be a perfectly beautiful relationship that reflects His essence, which is perfect intimacy. As the song expresses, God is the only One who can help our broken hearts come together because the only way our marriage will last is if we are "broken together"!

If it's good for our marriage, then it's good for both of us!

As we change our focus to living out a relationship *with* each other, striving for its intended intimacy, we will face obstacles along the way—obstacles that can be and must be battled together, with God and each other.

Bitterness from old and new wounds will try to prevail, but we have the power and strength to overcome.

Our differences, natural and learned, will also threaten to defeat us. But, again, through knowledge, which leads to grace and wisdom, we will be victorious together.

And when we share our brokenness with each other, our mingled tears will bring us one step closer to perfect intimacy!

REFLECTION

Wives, it is your turn to plan a "conversation date" that includes a time and place that is safe, comfortable and allows for intimate conversation. Each of you must do some research to come up with at least two created (that is, natural) differences between men and women and bring those to the date.

- First ask the two basic questions:
  "What was great this past week?"
  "What was difficult this past week?"
- Then have a fun and honest dialogue about your differences based on the research statements you brought along. Are they true for you two? Is it new information? Have they created problems in your relationship? Do you need to validate each other in those differences, work together to create healthy responses to what can't be changed, and eliminate excuses when they can be?
- Find a location where people won't be staring at your tears and listen to the song "Broken Together." Talk about a time when the words rang true in your relationship.

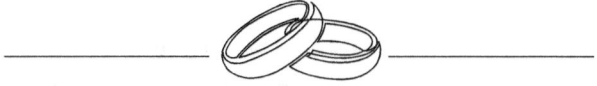

CHAPTER 10

INTIMACY LIVED OUT

WHEN THE TWO OF US GO OUT for a dinner date, more often than not, we are seated at a table that can accommodate four. The challenge is, after Diane is seated, as to where I (Mike) should sit. The goal for a date is to create a setting that promotes connection—such as conversation, holding hands and even stealing food off of each other's plate. So I will sit beside her rather than across from her. Sometimes when we sit together on the same side of a booth, we can almost feel the stares of other diners, as if we are an anomaly. But if the point of our date is to be together, why would we want any more physical separation than necessary?

They say that you can spot a married couple on a date because they're the ones ignoring each other. The truth is, it's not about whether the couple is married or not; rather, it is if they have learned the art of being intimate. That's our focus in the next two chapters: the importance and joy of being intimate in your relationship with each other.

We asked the question in Chapter 3, "What is this thing called intimacy?" Hopefully we stressed the importance of it to the point that there is no doubt that an epic marriage cannot exist without it. God's design for marriage calls for perfect intimacy!

One of the follow-up questions focused on the different types of intimacy. We identified five common types as emotional, spiritual, intellectual, social and physical. Then we briefly defined them. But what does it look like to live out each one of those within the marriage relationship, including how we approach them as a husband/male and a wife/female?

EMOTIONAL INTIMACY

In a recent counseling session with a husband, he made the statement that he *felt* like his wife didn't find him attractive anymore. He was confused with the follow-up question: "How did that make you feel?" Thinking he hadn't spoken loudly enough, he made the same comment with more volume. He was even more confused when we asked the question again. When he rephrased his statement, with the same result, in desperation he asked what he wasn't understanding.

A light bulb went on when we asked how the *thought* he was expressing made him *feel*. Was he sad or angry or frustrated? Not surprisingly, he had a hard time figuring out what his true *feelings* were. We spent the next few minutes explaining the difference between thoughts, opinions and feelings—and significantly more time explaining the need for self-intimacy in order to get connected with his feelings.

We create emotional intimacy when we honestly share all that is going on inside of our heads and our hearts. But we can't do that unless we know all that we are thinking, feeling and believing. We won't do that if we have been taught that we're not supposed to do that. We also won't do that if we believe it is unsafe to do so.

We briefly alluded to the fact that we have a son who died. Ryan was born with anencephaly, and he only lived for a short period of time. We didn't find out about his condition until shortly before he was born. And because our regular doctor was out of town, we ended up receiving horrible advice from the on-call doctor. In our shock, we followed his direction and ended up never seeing or holding Ryan. To this day we don't know where he was when he took his last breath or who was with him.

Over the years, our intimacy has grown significantly as we have shared our thoughts, our feelings and our broken dreams with each other. But it didn't start out that way! We were two individuals experiencing the worst possible pain with no clue what to do with it. In our naïveté, we expected and assumed that the other one felt the same. The advice we received from good-intentioned friends and family only made things worse.

Grieving is a very lonely experience, and the stages of grief are not linear, making them very confusing. We had to embrace being intimate with our own self so that we could first understand our own feelings, which often required us to stop long enough to feel them. Then we had to choose to become transparent and vulnerable so that we could experience the freedom we needed to grieve. We learned that, to be emotionally intimate, we had to really listen to each other's journey. We had to not only hear what our spouse was saying but also validate the other's feelings and share the pain.

Mike's Story

One of the struggles I had to deal with was the cultural standard that men don't cry. Then add to that my experience growing up when I was told that I was "too sensitive" when I did cry. Early on in our marriage, Diane walked on eggshells whenever I shut down because I didn't want to be "too sensitive." My silence felt like punishment to her, and it sometimes was because that's what I learned from my dad as I grew up. A big adjustment for me was allowing myself to feel and realizing that, with Diane, I was safe to share those feelings. Today, I embrace my sensitive spirit, believing it is part of God's unique design of me.

Diane's Story

We came into the loss of Ryan in a weakened state. I was sick through most of the pregnancy. During that time, we built a house and had just moved in a few weeks before Ryan was due. I was in survival mode, just getting through each day. When I found out that the baby I had carried for nine months was going to die, I shut down. Instead of getting the help we needed, we tried to do it alone. As a result, we became farther apart. We didn't go through it *with* each other. We weren't safe to share our pain because we weren't safe to feel our pain. We tried to avoid the grief we felt, hoping in time it would just go away, not realizing it was coming out sideways and against each other. I grew up believing you shouldn't dwell on negative feelings. That made others uncomfortable. Growing up with a father who had cancer, I watched him deny the possibility of death even though it was imminent. Even though I feared losing him, it was never discussed. I knew how to shut those feelings down, so I did it again when I buried my son.

This division later turned into intimacy as we each connected with our own self, learned to share our thoughts and feelings with one another, and walked in each other's grief.

Our emotional intimacy created a ripple effect as well, giving both of our daughters the freedom to process their emotions and their own grief. Kate was four years old when Ryan died and was following our lead to be strong and move on. It wasn't until many years later that she was able to express her anger and sorrow that we never brought a baby home from the hospital. She took on a great responsibility of not causing us anymore pain at the expense of feeling her own.

Molly, who was born 19 months after Ryan died, came into this world believing she was responsible for bringing joy back into our household. It also took years before she was able to experience her own grief because she was supposed to have a big brother to watch over her.

Many tears have been shed by the four of us over the past few years as it seems that the more we understand the importance of emotional intimacy, the more we have grown in it. It also has become a foundational part of our marriage relationship. Here's a treasure we have also experienced as a result: the laughter has exponentially increased along with the tears because, as we learn to share grief, we also became better at sharing joy. Sorrow is divided and joy is multiplied through emotional intimacy!

Emotional intimacy takes a lot of work (mostly on one's self) and requires taking a great risk due to our fear of rejection. But the greater risk is holding back, which prevents us from the joy of being one with each other.

SPIRITUAL INTIMACY

There is no order of importance to the five types of intimacy, but without emotional intimacy, spiritual intimacy would probably be lacking as well. Again, it requires taking a great risk to share our relationship with God because it is so unique to us.

We experience spiritual intimacy when we explore and share our inner beliefs, values and philosophical views and work together to find the truth. Having said that, our intent is not to give you a model of how to achieve spiritual intimacy in your marriage. Rather, we thought we would share some wisdom from our own experience and observations.

Here's the first piece of wisdom: Not unlike emotional intimacy, you can't be spiritually intimate with each other without first being intimate with God individually.

We have worked with a number of couples over the years where one or both partners were not pursuing a relationship with God. I (Mike) had to make a difficult decision years ago to tell a couple that I couldn't officiate their wedding. I would be causing and accepting a lie when I asked the groom if he was ready to enter into a covenant marriage knowing he did not have a relationship with God. I desperately desired to disciple him in his faith journey for the sake of their marriage relationship, but he was unwilling. I knew that the bride's idea that she had enough faith for both of them didn't work either. I have lost track of this couple since then, and I hope they are doing well. But I know that by design they have limited their joy if they still lack spiritual intimacy.

For us, our "religious" experience growing up was very similar to each other's. We both also had the revelation days apart that we are created to walk in God's love, not strive to earn it. Fortunately, we were both committed from that day forward to seek that intimacy both individually and together.

If you or your spouse is not in relationship with God, we encourage you to seek spiritual direction and persevere, praying God will unite you in this journey. However, we also know that a relationship with God, individually and as a couple, is unique.

When we ask individuals and couples what they believe spiritual intimacy looks like, we have realized from their answers that many (including us) have experienced a linear teaching with regard to growing in intimacy with God. "Do these five things, in this order, at this time of day, and you will be one with God." The problem is, that model doesn't take into account our uniqueness or our season of life. For us, it had the opposite impact due to the guilt we experienced when we didn't get up early to read our Bible because we had been up half the night with a newborn or had an early meeting to attend.

We believe that Jesus is the way, the truth and the light (John 14:6), but we also believe there are many ways to experience His presence. We heard a message one day that asked the question, "Why would our infinite Father create a finite path to intimacy with Him?" We have incorporated that idea into our individual intimacy with God and our spiritual intimacy with each other, which allows us to operate out of desire to be with Him rather than believing He will be angry with us if we don't.

One more gem of wisdom: It is not about doing the same things or doing things together; rather, it is about continually sharing your individual revelation with each other.

In the season of life that the two of us are in, our spiritual journeys have a lot of similarities. Both of us start our day with a cup of coffee and one-on-one time with God. There is usually one devotional we are both reading, as well as time spent journaling, reading the Bible, listening to God and sharing our needs/desires. We are not, however, in the same room, reading all the same books, or following the same format. Still, we are both connecting with God. And although it is deeply intimate and personal, we are always anxious to share our thoughts and experience with each other—to create spiritual unity.

What's exciting is that it doesn't stop with the two of us. Some of our favorite times with our kids are the times we spend around the dinner table when one of us shares a recent experience with God or the impact a book has had on our understanding of Him. What's exciting to observe is that as the grandkids get older, they are not as anxious to leave the table to go play. The joy we share with each other through our conversation is contagious.

Our individual relationships with God are unique, but it doesn't seem to require any risk to share it with each other because we know how beneficial it is to our marriage!

The final thought on spiritual intimacy is this: When combined with emotional intimacy, it will connect you in a place you may not have realized existed.

We have wept together when we have experienced great loss in our life. Sharing that sorrow draws us into a deep place together. We have also experienced such great moments of joy that they cause us to wrap our arms around each other and again shed lots of tears. If someone was observing those moments of great joy, they would probably have a lot of compassion for us, thinking we were extremely sad.

What we have learned is that both the deep sorrow and the deep joy go to the same place in our soul—the place where we are one with God. And because we are together in that, we are one with each other. It's spiritual intimacy. Hallelujah!

"...love the Lord your God with all your heart and with all your soul and with all your mind and with all your strength." (Mark 12:30)

And do it together!

INTELLECTUAL INTIMACY

Although emotional intimacy focuses on feelings and emotions, intellectual intimacy is the sharing of opinions, thoughts, ideas and interests. It is connecting brain to brain versus heart to heart. Our parenting style, our finances, where we live and how we manage our household are all areas we need to be united in and seek agreement, which requires intellectual intimacy.

It is interesting that the two of us met years ago while working for the same company and in the same field. A few years later, because we shared the same value of raising our two girls with a stay-at-home mother, our "careers" were different—managing the household versus the corporate world. Then, many years later, we found ourselves again working together in the completely different field of counseling. Throughout the whole time, we always maintained a connection intellectually even when so much of our time was spent going in different directions.

Without purposely trying, we always had (and have) an appreciation for the other's opinions, ideas and interests, even when they weren't the same. They mostly were (are). Our value systems don't align when it comes to the type of fiction books that we read or our favorite color. The genre of music in our cars is different as well. However, when it comes to core values, we have never been significantly apart. Even where we go on vacation, or what we do when we get there, is seldom a difficult decision because our ideas and interests align.

In our early days of dating, we were seldom apart. During that time together, we made it a point to learn about each other and to share our past experiences. We were so connected from the beginning that we can't remember a moment when we decided "maybe we should get married." It was just kind of assumed from the beginning.

One of the decisions we made early on in our marriage was to make it a priority at the beginning of each year to create time and space to intentionally share our hopes and expectations for the coming year as individuals and as a family. It was fun to dream together, and it created a partnership in prayer and focus.

I (Mike) enjoy designing the layout of a space to make it functional. But what people notice when they enter our home or counseling center is the warmth and beauty that Diane creates with her decorating ability. Over the years we have done a lot of projects—built homes, remodeled basements, etc.—and we have enjoyed the creating process. One of our biggest projects was remodeling the space for our counseling center, which, looking back, was a huge undertaking. It was a joy to do because we were moving together toward the same goal, the same dream. We also appreciated each other's talents and gifts.

We can't remember many instances when we weren't connected in our opinions and dreams. But there was one…

Our Story

We had recently moved into our current house and were in the process of making it a home. I (Diane) brought up the idea that we should remodel our kitchen. Mike quickly responded that we couldn't afford to. That ended the discussion—until I brought it up again and heard the same response. What I pointed out to Mike was that I knew we couldn't afford to at that moment, but I was sharing a dream, and he was squashing it. I wanted him to dream with me.

I (Mike) realized that I was operating out of fear and Diane was operating out of desire. I quickly began dreaming as well (which resulted in the remodeling of our kitchen a short time later).

We are intellectually intimate when we are safe to voice our thoughts, ideas and opinions and when we value the perspective of our spouse, even when it is different. But it also requires us to have a desire to seek truth, which we can find faster together than alone.

SOCIAL INTIMACY

What is our favorite social activity that we do together? That question came up the other day, and neither of us had an answer. We both had a list of things that we agreed we enjoy doing together, but there wasn't one that stood out above the rest. We also both agreed that there were activities neither one of us enjoy together or apart. What became clear in the conversation is that we just love being together!

A significant memory that surfaced for me (Mike) during the discussion was a hike up Long's Peak in Colorado. The hike started before dawn in order for us to be back below a certain elevation by a certain time due to the risk of thunderstorms. It wasn't a particularly grueling climb except for the altitude and the field of boulders near the top. The view at the top of the peak was spectacular, and as I stood there taking it all in, I had one vivid thought: *As great as this accomplishment is, it lacks joy—because Diane isn't here to share it with.* As I hiked back down with my boss and co-worker to prepare for a corporate gathering, I wondered if it was even worth the effort.

We would choose to be together at home just watching a movie over experiencing something majestic without the other. Oneness doesn't happen through the sharing of a picture of a beautiful sunset, but it does happen when we create a memory together. Remember the beautiful anniversary dinner we mentioned earlier? What a wonderful memory! But it was followed by encountering a tropical storm and the difficult process of trying to get back home. After hours in airports and driving through flooded streets, we arrived home one hour before we were originally scheduled even though we left two days early. But even that is a memory that created intimacy *because we were together, focused on the same common interest*!

Please understand that we are not recommending that a couple has to be together 24/7. In fact, it is healthy for our self-intimacy to figure out what activities "fill us up" and to give ourselves—and each other—permission to do those regularly. That also adds to our intimacy with each other.

And although it is great to enjoy time with another couple or group participating in social events, make sure that you prioritize and intentionally set aside time for just the two of you!

Social intimacy is about spending time together and experiencing common interests. But the emphasis is on doing it together.

(Physical intimacy is the last of the five types of intimacy to explore. And because it is much more challenging to create and maintain, we have made it a chapter of its own.)

"Therefore a man shall leave his father and his mother and hold fast to his wife, and they shall become one flesh." (Genesis 2:24)

God's design for marriage cannot exist without intimacy—with our own self, with Him and then with each other. But intimacy requires risk, the risk of being rejected. Although that is possible with many relationships other than marriage, the fear of rejection should never be present in a covenant relationship.

Therefore, one of the mandates as a husband and wife within the sacrament of marriage is to create a safe environment in which, barring extreme circumstances, the fear of one leaving does not exist—and the desire to pursue greater and greater intimacy is always present.

Creating emotional intimacy means we have to be in touch with our own feelings and transparent enough to share them with our spouse. Spiritual intimacy requires us to pursue God and His revelations in our life and be excited about sharing them with each other. Intellectual intimacy and social intimacy bring constant excitement into our relationship as we create and pursue dreams with a like-minded partner.

And when we make intimacy a priority and do the work required to build and maintain it, we become *one* with each other and with God. Then we draw upon the reward of joy He has promised us!

REFLECTION

Make a list of the top five activities you and your spouse enjoy together. Then plan out a date for each activity on your list.

If your list doesn't include a romantic dinner together, add that to your list. At that dinner, you can do the following:

- First ask the two basic questions:
  "What did I do that blessed you this week?"
  "What did I do that created difficulty for you?"
- Google "date night questions for married couples" and find a list of questions or a book with questions to bring along. Take turns picking questions to ask and answer throughout your meal.
- Look around the restaurant at the other couples and see if you can figure out who is married and who is dating. (Make sure your phones only get answered if the babysitter calls so other couples won't know you're married!)

Separately spend some time evaluating your intimacy level in the four categories of emotional, spiritual, intellectual and social. Then find an uninterrupted time when you can share your thoughts with each other. Make a plan to improve any areas that you consider weak.

CHAPTER 11

LET'S TALK SEX

ONE OF THE GREAT ATTRIBUTES THAT EVERYONE appreciated about Diane's mom was her strong faith, followed closely by her sense of humor. You couldn't let your guard down for a second or you would find yourself sitting on a whoopee cushion or being handed a raw chicken gizzard. She was always entertaining at family gatherings.

One of her favorite lines was "Let's talk sex." And it was not because it was a topic she wanted to discuss; rather, it *always* halted conversations that were starting to get a little too controversial. We always knew when she said it that we needed to consider changing the subject.

She grew up in an era where conversations about sex were held in private. Talking about sex was taboo and uncomfortable. The reality is that not much has changed. Even today, if you ask a couple what their most difficult conversations are about, the answer is often "sex."

That wasn't always the case. In the beginning, "... the man and his wife were both naked and were not ashamed" (Genesis 2:25). But then man chose knowledge over life, his will over God's will, his desires over God's design. As a result, "...they heard the sound of the Lord God walking in the garden in the cool of the day, and the man and his wife hid themselves from the presence of the Lord God among the trees of the garden. But the Lord God called to the man and said to him, 'Where are you?' And he said, 'I heard the sound of you in the garden, and I was afraid, because I was naked, and I hid myself'" (Genesis 3: 8–10).

Perhaps the difficulty of having conversations about sex has existed for thousands of years, and likely will for many more. But for now, setting aside our discomfort…

LET'S TALK SEX!
(And Physical Intimacy)

In the previous chapter we shared some of our wisdom on how to live out four of the five types of intimacy in your marriage relationship: emotional, intellectual, spiritual and social. We left the fifth type, *physical intimacy*, as a chapter unto itself. The reality is that it could be a book unto itself. If you search for books on physical intimacy on Amazon, thousands of results will come up. So, one chapter will hardly scratch the surface. Still, we wanted to emphasize its importance in a properly beautiful marriage as well as share some thoughts related to how we should and shouldn't approach it.

All four types of intimacy discussed in Chapter 10 are important to create and foster with your spouse. We believe they need to be developed to a great degree before you enter into the marriage covenant and before engaging in sexual physical intimacy.

What's also true is that we can experience one or all of the other four types in other relationships, such as with our kids, extended family or those whom we work with. We can, and should (with permission), also experience non-sexual physical intimacy with others in our life. It's been determined that physical touch is important for our well-being, and it has even been proven through research that an infant's growth is healthier when the child regularly experiences the loving touch of another.

Per God's design, however, the fifth type of intimacy, specifically the sexual part of physical intimacy, should only be experienced with the one person you have committed to be with in a covenant marriage relationship. It is the culmination of creating emotional, intellectual, spiritual and social intimacy. It is also probable that entering into physical intimacy prior to establishing the other four may hinder your ability to create strong connections emotionally and spiritually.

Physical intimacy is both affection and sexual activity. Affection doesn't necessarily lead to sex and should be regularly given and received. On the other hand, sex should always incorporate affection. Sex also should be a regular part of our marriage relationship.

Because sex is unique to the marriage relationship, our primary focus for the rest of this chapter is on the sexual intimacy part of experiencing an epic marriage.

~~PHYSICAL~~ SEXUAL INTIMACY

Mike's Story
I was probably 11 or 12 years old when my dad had the sex conversation with me. But it wasn't really a conversation. It was him taking me to a father/son gathering at the YMCA where they showed us a film strip (back before the days of videos) and may have imparted some teaching to a room full of naïve young men. I don't remember much, except for walking out of there wondering what I had just learned. Maybe my dad asked me if I had any questions on the ride home, but I don't think I even knew what questions to ask. I'm pretty sure the topic never came up again. So in my formative years, sex was confusing.

In seventh or eighth grade the subject was brought up in health class, with the males and females separated, of course. By then I had a better understanding of how it took place, but the teacher certainly didn't provide any guidance on its purpose, along with the potential consequences of pregnancy and sexually transmitted diseases. The pleasure of sex was a topic of conversation that happened on the playground. Then the church brought in the moral aspect of it, and I knew that I was going to rot in hell if I didn't wait until marriage because sex outside of marriage was bad!

All in all, I was a confused, fearful, shame-avoiding teenager—and I wasn't alone.

As for Diane, she grew up attending parochial schools and didn't even get the film strip. It was just avoided altogether!

Things are not a lot different today.

Even though it was somewhat awkward, we tried to make sure our two daughters grew up with a healthy understanding of sex and its purpose—at least to the best of our ability since we ourselves were still growing in the knowledge and the beauty of sexual intimacy as created by God.

Sex became a significant topic in our epic marriage teaching, which led to much research, many conversations and lots of questions during the workshops we facilitated. And in the course of that work, our discomfort when talking about sexual intimacy lessened significantly while our desire to create a strong and lasting connection of physical intimacy grew considerably.

Prior to that research, we may have never had a healthy conversation about the purpose of sex in a marriage. Because the sexual revolution happened before we married, we entered into sexual activity with a worldly understanding that was focused on pleasure. Our bedroom door was closed to keep others out, including God.

WHAT SEX IS

The joy increased significantly when we realized that God has given us sex for the purpose of physical intimacy—to become "one," literally.

When we focus on His design for sexual relations, we connect physically, emotionally and spiritually. It is fun, has the potential for great pleasure, and binds us together through the release of hormones. Then, to top it all off, new life can be created as a result!

Sex is an amazing gift created by and given to us by God, to be freely enjoyed within the marriage relationship with gratitude!

WHAT SEX IS NOT

In our 45 years of marriage, we never experienced a time when we thought physical intimacy wasn't important. Even though we didn't fully understand its purpose, we knew we wanted our marriage to always incorporate a healthy sex life. When we started counseling couples, we were both very surprised at how many couples did not regularly engage in sexual intercourse and how many had not had sexual relations for months or years. Through the course of our work with these couples, we gained a great understanding of the importance and purpose of sex, as well as what sex isn't.

Sex Is Not bad

Over the years we have counseled newlyweds as well as couples that have been married for more than 50 years with regard to the statement that resonates in the back of their mind: sex is bad. That line was most likely embedded there through a religious teaching when they were teenagers. Both of us heard that in youth group, as did our daughters and their husbands.

What starts out as a spiritual teaching with good intent—"sex outside of the boundaries of marriage is wrong"—becomes a mind issue as the mind captures the lie that sex is bad. It is a classic example of what happens when we continually focus on the sinfulness of something instead of focusing on the amazing creation that it is.

The work we suggest individuals do is change the narrative. Renounce the lie that sex is bad and replace it with the statement that "God created sex as a beautiful act between a husband and wife to enhance our oneness." Repeat it, praise Him for it and be grateful for the gift that it is!

However, we cannot ignore those who have been abused sexually. It is very difficult to see sex as the creation it is designed to be when the experience we have had was horrible. Again, we have to change the narrative from the mindset that "sex is bad" to the truth that "how someone used it for their selfish pleasure" was bad.

Statistically, the number of people who have been sexually abused is staggering, and that abuse most often happens to women because men are physically stronger. We highly recommend seeking counseling if you have experienced sexual abuse, and we want to encourage you that healing is possible. Our hope is that you can experience gratitude for the creation that it is with the one you were designed to experience it with!

Sex Is Not a Weapon

God didn't design sex for the benefit of one spouse over the other. It is supposed to be good for your marriage, for both of you. Yet, so often, because of bitterness, one spouse withholds physical intimacy (sexual as well as non-sexual) as retaliation against the other—and deprives him or herself of joy as well!

It is stated very clearly in scripture that we should not deprive each other of sexual relations, unless agreed upon for a period of prayer and fasting (1 Corinthians 7:5). When we do, we are partnering with the evil one instead of with God and each other, with whom we are to stand and fight for an epic marriage.

If physical intimacy is not a regular part of your marriage, we encourage you to review the guide to removing bitterness in Appendix A, seek counsel for the cause of your bitterness, and celebrate the joy that sex is intended to be.

Sex was never intended to be a way to manipulate each other. The idea that one of us "needs sex" to relieve stress or needs the spouse to perform a certain sexual act is pure selfishness. In the same way, if we are doing it to get something in return, the whole focus has changed the marriage into one of contract versus covenant. Our *marriage* needs us to have sex regularly with agreement on what is involved in the act of lovemaking.

Sex Should Never Be in Fear

"If I don't have sex with him tonight, he will be angry." "If I suggest we have sex tonight, I risk rejection if she says 'no.'" Those are two very common thoughts that we hear from wives and husbands, the root of which is fear. God didn't create sex to contain the emotion of fear. But because our sexual intimacy requires work to get to agreement on when, where and what, it often seems easier to operate out of a contract instead of a covenant. The focus again is on what is best for "me" instead of what is best for the marriage. The thought that one's expectation might not be met creates fear.

That fear often turns into manipulation because, if one partner operates in fear, the power to control the actions belongs to the other. And if that partner is focusing on his or her own pleasure, rather than pleasuring the spouse, the when, where and how become that partner's to control.

Sex and sexual acts should never be unsafe or done without agreement!

Sex Should Not Contain Expectations

It should not contain expectations, except for two. First, if physically possible, sex should be a regular part of the marriage. We are programmed by culture to believe sex is best when it is spontaneous. There is nothing wrong with that, but as we go through different seasons of life, there is often little room for spontaneity. The solution to that is not to be patient, but rather to make regular sex a priority in our schedule. Although that may sound sterile, it isn't. To agree that what is best for the marriage is to create time and space for sexual intimacy at least "x" times per week, and that knowing the most opportune time is "x" or "y" is actually freeing and worth figuring out. It is surprising how many couples begin enjoying a regular sex life when they incorporate planning into the process.

I (Mike) knew we had gotten to a much healthier place in our sexual intimacy when Diane asked how many times I expected to have sex while we were enjoying a long weekend getaway. My response surprised both of us as I realized I was no longer operating out of expectation, but rather desire, which gave freedom to both of us to enjoy our time together without fear or manipulation.

The second expectation is that we will agree upon what is included in our sexual activity. It is great to experiment and explore what creates pleasure for each other, but it must be safe to do so. Again, that requires openness in our communication, in which we trust that both of us will clearly communicate and will listen when the other shares. Assuming that our spouse will find a certain act pleasurable, and then getting upset when he or she doesn't, creates an atmosphere of fear.

Sex Does Not Exclude Pleasure

To reiterate, experiencing physical pleasure while we are fulfilling our purpose of creating sexual intimacy is an amazing part of God's creation. To that end, we have the ability to enhance that experience by knowing what creates pleasure for our own body and for our spouse—and openly and unashamedly sharing that. Of the thousands of books that are available on physical intimacy, a good number contain ideas of how to enhance our sexual pleasure and at the same time honor how God created us.

Again, sexual acts should never be unsafe or done without agreement! Some of the greatest moments of intimacy result when we try something different and end up (unhurt) on the floor, laughing!

When was the last time you laughed while making love and neither one of you was offended? That's when you know your sexual intimacy is pretty healthy.

An easy way to wrap up this section on what *sex is not* is to simply remind ourselves that if it isn't creating intimacy, we are not operating per God's design. False teachings, revenge, fear, manipulation, unrealistic expectations or lack of knowledge *cannot* result in intimacy. If we are not participating in the act of lovemaking out of desire and passion, giving of ourselves freely, we are missing out on a significant part of the oneness God intends for an epic marriage!

WHAT WE MUST UNDERSTAND

We cannot stress enough that men and women are different, both by design and by experience. When it comes to enhancing our sexual intimacy, we must understand what some of those differences are. Most men, for example, do not understand why their wife isn't thinking about sex as often as they are. In fact, they often believe that their wife is! The reality is that their wife is flabbergasted that the husband thinks about it so much!

We have found through counseling others and through our own experience that, through faulty teaching and negative experiences, we often operate in sexual unhealthiness to one degree or another. We need to examine ourselves—body, mind and spirit, and as a man or a woman—and compare what we think to God's design in order to eliminate sexual unhealthiness.

We then need to seek to understand our spouse's design as well, and we must appreciate our differences to create intimacy rather than destroy it. It is a never-ending dialogue of learning about each other and trying to figure out God's reasons for our differences. Maybe He intends it to be a never-ending conversation. That alone may be the reason He made us different; He knew that in order to fulfill our purpose of intimacy, we had to *talk sex*. And if we could do that well, then all of the other dialogues that we need to have about finances, kids, in-laws, etc. would be easy.

The differences are numerous, and we encourage you to explore some of the resources focused on them Then have intentional conversations about them. But here are a couple of examples of how men and women are different to get you started with your conversation.

Physical Differences

A wooden peg and a dowel hole provide a strong joint between two pieces of wood. It's interesting that God designs us to be connected sexually in much the same way—which is a connection much stronger than just the two of us abutting each other. So maybe He knew what He was doing when He created us!

Of course, He did (and does), but don't we sometimes wonder? For example, on average, a woman has a lower sex drive than a man (and most say they would change that if they could). Without getting into all of the physical reasons related to hormones such as testosterone and estrogen, suffice it to say that our levels are different based on what our bodies need for healthy development, and our sex drives are different because of it.

But just maybe God created our sex drives to be different so that we *had* to talk about it in order to get to a place of agreement on what is best for our marriage. He didn't create us differently to cause division, but rather to increase connection. So we have to figure out and trust His why.

Men are much more visual than women. Research shows that 98% of men will notice when an attractive woman enters the room (they can't help it) because of the wiring in a specific part of their brain.[1] A woman's brain does not react the same way. (Note: It is what a man does *after* he notices that is important!)

God created man this way. We can believe that it was a mistake until we realize He had a purpose related to pursuing our wife and being stimulated by her beauty, which is a good thing. But while there is much visual stimulation in our culture today, a man's ability to manage the temptation can still prevail since God also provides the way out.

Speaking as a man with this natural trait, I (Mike) am relieved to know that my instinct to notice an attractive woman is from God and that I need to be aware so that I can use it as He intended. My work is to control my thoughts after I notice. One friend shared that the way he does this is to say, "She's not my wife."

A woman's appearance is important to her as well. For a wife, it is helpful to understand that her husband's instinct to notice is not the problem if he maintains pure thoughts. Nor does it diminish her attraction in his eyes. A woman desires that her husband thinks she's beautiful, and despite how she may sometimes respond, she is positively impacted when he tells her so.

On the other hand, a man's appearance is not that sexually stimulating to his wife. But because physical appearance is important to him, he assumes his wife should be stimulated by his appearance, and his self-esteem is wounded when she doesn't respond as "she should." Understanding that is helpful, as well as understanding that she can just as easily be discouraged when a man doesn't take care of himself through poor hygiene, sloppiness, etc.

Emotional Differences

It's often said that men give love to get sex and women give sex to get love. That doesn't sound properly beautiful. But if we explore it a little, there is some merit behind the saying.

Oxytocin is a chemical messenger in the brain that impacts men and women in different ways and amounts. It is often referred to as the bonding hormone, or love hormone, and is released in both men and women during and after sex. It creates connection—again, it is part of God's amazing creation of us and of sexual intimacy.

One researcher put forth the idea that the release of oxytocin in a male is enhanced through physical touch and fosters emotional intimacy. For a female, emotional connection prior to physical touch enhances her release of oxytocin during sex.[2]

We have experienced that in our marriage when life has preempted our time set aside for sexual intimacy. Both of us will notice that we are just "feeling disconnected" as a result. I (Mike) start to disconnect emotionally without the physical touch, while Diane's desire to connect physically begins to wane.

In other words, regular physical intimacy (both sexual and non-sexual) is important in bonding to each other and confirms the reason God designed marriage to be the only relationship that should include sexual intimacy.

Mindset Differences

Mike's Story

After 45 years of marriage, I am still gaining understanding of my wife—both in general as a woman and uniquely as Diane. I've realized that I need to be intentional in studying her, and each time I learn something new, I am more grateful for who she is. She would say the same about me.

Throughout our marriage, we have made it a priority to take time for our marriage and get away for a weekend. Though the "windows" in the "computer screen" of Diane's mind never completely close, these weekends allowed her to at least minimize some of them, such as the kids, the house, her clients, etc. It allowed us to focus on our relationship with limited interruption.

I planned the weekends so she didn't have to open another window. But prior to fully understanding God's design, I entered into them with romantic expectations. One getaway was almost ruined because I didn't realize the extent of the emotional concern she was carrying for others, and I was not allowing her time to release some of those responsibilities because she has the mind and heart of a woman and the God-given gift of compassion. I have come to understand that, because a woman is created to have greater qualities for nurturing and comforting, Diane naturally carries a high volume of concern for our kids, our grandkids, the serenity of our home, and me. Add in her compassion for her clients struggling in a chaotic world and our friends who are aging and experiencing health problems, and her mind is continually full and trying to find space for more.

Our hearts are similar in that we both walk daily through life's struggles and challenges with the people God has placed in our life. But our minds are different in that Diane doesn't fully release one to focus on another, while my thoughts are on one at a time.

I have finally realized that she is not supposed to be like me—and that I shouldn't try to "fix" her because she is authentic in who God created her to be. What I am trying to get better at is telling her how much I appreciate her, who she is and what she does.

Recognizing how our minds are different is highly important in our sexual intimacy. A man's mind is often focused on sex, and he would change that if he could. A woman's mind has to work at focusing on sexual intimacy, and she would change that if she could.

So, men, the next time you ask your wife to engage sexually, and she says, "no," it's not because she's not interested or doesn't find you attractive. It's because she has too many thoughts running through her mind, is exhausted from caring for so many, and could probably use some emotional connection before her body is able to catch up. But don't give up asking because your pride is hurt; instead, help her close some of her "windows" and connect with and validate her emotions. In the words of a friend of ours: "You don't have a right to her body until you have taken good care of her soul!"

Here's a list of differences you can put in your nightstands as a reminder:

Some Facts about Women:
- She has a lower sex drive than you, and she'd change that if she could.
- She needs more warm-up time than you.
- Your body (no matter how much of a stud you are) does not by itself turn on her body.
- For her, sex starts in her heart. Her body's ability to respond to you sexually is tied to how she feels emotionally about you at the moment.
- She wants pleasure as much as you do, and if it's not happening, she may be reluctant.
- With sex, her "no" doesn't mean you!

Some Facts about Men:
- Sex is often on his mind, but it's not always about sex.
- Sex fills a powerful emotional need.

- Fulfilling sex makes him feel loved and desired (it says he is more important to you than anything else in the world).
- Fulfilling sex gives him confidence.
- He wants to be wanted.
- He struggles with rejection if you don't want to have sex or are responding out of duty.

Physical intimacy is a beautiful gift, created by God, to enhance a properly beautiful marriage relationship. It is designed to be received, understood, appreciated and used as He intended, not as the worldly culture portrays it. Throughout history, mankind has failed to focus on the purpose of sex and, in the process, has limited the joy and physical pleasure that is available to us when we follow His design.

And because we are so different in our physical, emotional and mindset differences, it requires a great deal of intentional learning to understand and agree how sex can and should be a part of our fully becoming one and experiencing the joy of an epic marriage!

We do want to note that often physical problems or emotional pain will keep us from fully experiencing God's gift of physical intimacy. If you haven't already done so, we encourage you to seek medical and emotional guidance to try to gain whatever healing is possible.

REFLECTION

This should come as no surprise, but you need to have an open and honest dialogue with your spouse about your physical intimacy. It might be an uncomfortable conversation, but being intentional about it will make it easier over time. Here are some questions to get you started. And remember, like your other intentional conversations, *listen*, learn and don't get defensive!

- After reading this chapter, what new understanding do you have about God's design for sexual intimacy?
- What needs to change to enhance your connection sexually?
- If it hasn't been highly important in your marriage, how can you make it a priority to have sex regularly? How often

and when would be best for your marriage? What can you do to help each other create that time and space?

- What is and isn't enjoyable when you engage physically (sexually and non-sexually)? What would you like to try, and would you feel safe doing so?
- Give it a go!

If there are any problems or issues that haven't been resolved that keep you from sexual intimacy, go immediately to the next chapter, which is focused on conflict resolution.

CHAPTER 12

RESOLVING CONFLICT

AT A RECENT BOXING MATCH OF TWO well-known fighters, the asking price for a ringside seat was $21,000. The payout was rumored to have been $40 million for the winner and $20 million for the loser. For fighting! It would seem that the world loves a good fight.

Now imagine this...the bell sounds, and two fighters come charging out of their respective corners till they are going toe to toe in the middle of the ring. The one in the red trunks takes a mighty swing and lands a ferocious blow to the right cheek of the one in the blue trunks. The man in blue staggers back from the impact, shakes his head to clear the cobwebs, resets his balance, steps back into range of his opponent...and turns his left cheek for the man in red to hit as well (Matthew 5:39).

Can you imagine the boos that would resonate from those who paid big bucks to sit in the first row to watch a great conflict unfold? Can you imagine the promoters and sponsors racing for their phones to call their lawyers to file lawsuits? Can you imagine the surprise in the mind of the fighter in the red trunks—and probably disappointment—because he wanted to prove that he was the superior boxer?

We don't expect that scenario to ever unfold in the boxing ring. The purpose of the fight is to entertain, and the focus of the fighters is to win.

That "win at all costs" mindset is prevalent throughout our everyday life: in the board room, in politics, at the car dealership, in the grocery store checkout line, on the playground and in our fantasy football league. It often even exists in our relationships.

But what would the impact be if that "turn the other cheek" mentality happened within the arena of our marriage? What if our goal was not to win but to connect? And what if the "cost" of pursuing agreement was deep intimacy?

For a couple pursuing an epic marriage, that payout would be priceless!

"The gem cannot be polished without friction, nor man perfected without trials."

That quote from Seneca, a first century philosopher and playwright, is timeless and plays out every day in marriage. So maybe the art of intimacy in marriage is not about emotional or physical oneness but about a good fight?

We say that somewhat in jest, but the reality is that every significant relationship in our life will have conflict at some point, and the way we resolve it will either create separation or draw us closer together. Some would even say that healthy conflict can result in deep intimacy.

Conflict resolution is often the first topic couples want to talk about when they reach out for counseling. But until they both experience intimacy with self, with God and with each other, the ability to reach agreement through healthy conflict resolution will remain out of reach—and will cause separation rather than oneness.

The idea that healthy conflict can result in deep connection is true. We have experienced that in our own marriage over the years, suffering the consequences of unhealthy conflict resolution early on in our marriage as well as realizing the benefit of increased intimacy as we learned to resolve conflict properly.

We have also learned that the vast majority of couples who seek out marriage counseling have not figured out how to resolve conflict in a healthy way. Those hanging on to bitterness certainly have not, and those living in a contract marriage seldom will.

I (Mike) always start by asking this question: "What is the conflict resolution model that you use?" The answer is always some form of "we don't have one." But the truth is, we all do. It's the one we learned while growing up and watching our parents fight. Seldom is it the same as our spouse's, and it almost always is ineffective.

However, for those desiring and moving toward covenant relationship, intimacy through conflict is a reality. It involves having a system that incorporates common healthy *goals*, follows a process with *fundamental pieces* that both spouses understand and are committed to, and works within the *uniqueness of the individual personalities*.

THE GOALS

Seek Intimacy

Unlike the participants in a boxing or other sports match, the intent of conflict resolution in a covenant marriage relationship is not to win; rather, it is to create *intimacy* through *agreement*. We can get to agreement without creating intimacy, but we cannot create intimacy without first getting to agreement. *Our goal is always intimacy!*

Another question that we often ask couples when discussing healthy conflict is whether "compromise" is necessary to reach major decisions. The answer has always been "yes." But we don't agree. We explain that if one spouse gives in to the other, that's often thought of as a win/lose scenario, with the spouse who gets his or her way being declared the winner. It makes sense to them when we go on to explain that if one of them is giving in to the other, it can easily result in resentment or separation, in which case there is *no* winner.

Then there is always a confused look on their faces when we say that compromise is also lose/lose. Their thought is that each one walks away getting what he or she wants and feels like a winner. True. But what happens when sometime later both remember that they had to give up something in order to get what they wanted. Again, the result is most often resentment and separation, and thus it is lose/lose.

The only option left is agreement, which is *win/win*! Both are happy with the decision and neither had to give up something unwillingly.

Use the Correct Filter

What is critical in the process of reaching agreement is maintaining the correct filter. Remember that when we enter into a covenant agreement, our filter is no longer "what is best for me"; rather, it is "*what is best for our marriage*." Therefore, the best solution for resolving the conflict will be one that enhances our marriage and glorifies the One who created it. We will never find joy in something that might bring *us* happiness but causes unhappiness for our spouse.

Seek Godly Wisdom

Speaking of the One who created our marriage in the first place, our ability to reach an agreement that is best for our marriage is easy when we include God in the process! In our step-by-step process, we suggest that once we define the conflict—so that we're both on the same page—we spend time with God seeking the best solution. His desire is our intimacy with Him and each other. So if we both prayerfully seek wisdom, He will not give us two different solutions. Taking the time to pray not only allows the emotion to dissipate to a manageable level, but it also helps to simplify and streamline the whole process.

Heal and Connect

It would be easy to think that once we reach agreement, we would be finished. But remember that the goal is twofold: agreement *and* intimacy. They are distinct and equally important. It is worth repeating that we can't have intimacy without agreement, but we can reach agreement and still not have intimacy.

Think about it from the perspective of an injury. I (Mike) injured my ankle in college and ended up in a cast for a few weeks. I timed the removal of the cast with a job interview that I had, allowing myself 15 minutes to walk from the health center to the business school. I was 15 minutes late for the interview! The injury was healed, but there was so much stiffness in the surrounding area from being immobile that I could hardly walk. It was the most painful and slowest one-block journey I have experienced in my life.

Looking back, there was an expectation that the original injury would be healed—and it was. But never having had anything in a cast before, I failed to plan for the residual impact the original injury and healing process would have on the other parts of my body.

When the injury is minor and quick to heal, there is little to do but rip off the bandage and go on as if nothing happened. But when the injury is significant and the healing process is lengthy, we often require physical therapy to get all of the parts working correctly again.

The same is true with our conflict resolution. When the conflict is minor, intimacy often coincides with reaching agreement. But when the conflict is deep and painful, even after reaching agreement, there is a need for healing from the residual impact of the original injury.

Apologies, grace and forgiveness are all important in the healing process.

THE FUNDAMENTAL PIECES

Through our research and experience, we have created the Intimate Conflict Resolution (ICR) process as a step-by-step guide that couples can start with and modify over time as they learn what works best for them. The process is intended to be a tool a couple can use over and over in their marriage, one that becomes more and more effective with practice. It is a tool that can be modified and adapted to couples' circumstances as they grow together in intimacy. It is laid out in detail in Appendix B, but we wanted to share some thoughts here on a few fundamental pieces.

Validate

We were sitting on our couch, facing each other, working through a conflict, and not making much progress. It occurred to me (Diane) that we had neglected an important first step: *validation*. I asked Mike if he thought we had validated each other. Mike thought about it for a second and answered, "No, I don't. But if I validate your feelings, I'm admitting that I am wrong." Can you hear the sirens going off?

I (Mike) should have thought about it for a few more seconds before I answered because I clearly had missed the point of validation!)

When we validate the other person's feelings, we are stepping outside of our own emotion and connecting with our spouse's.

119

Regardless of whether we feel as if it was our mistake, to share with our partner, "I am so sorry you are feeling that pain! You are my wife/husband, and I never want you to feel that way," removes road-blocks—both ours and his or hers. When we hear those words, the defenses come down in both of us, and our starting point toward resolution aligns with our goal of agreement. It is no longer about "me" or the spouse, but about us.

Mindset

Early on in our marriage, we realized that we process differently. I (Diane) am an external processor; I try to figure things out by talking about it. The problem comes when I say things that can be taken as hurtful, even though that is not my intent. Mike processes internally, trying to figure out just the right way to share his feelings. If he doesn't communicate that he is doing that, it seems as if he has disengaged, which can also seem hurtful.

For us, we have had to work out a system that incorporates both of our process styles, thinking about the marriage first. We need to check our attitude before we engage. If we start out with a "win" instead of "connect" mindset, we will create division. Sometimes it is better to wait to engage than to engage with boxing gloves on. We have one rule, however, when one of us wants to delay the process. Any time we need to pause or need time to process first, we need to ask if the other is okay to wait, and we agree upon an acceptable time to reengage.

As we check and adjust ourselves, our purpose is to remember our goals of agreement and intimacy, determine if we are willing to validate the other, be vulnerable, *listen* and take responsibility for our actions.

Remember, our words can either create intimacy or cause divi-sion. If we begin with and maintain the proper mindset, the result can be greatly beneficial in aspiring toward an epic marriage!

Clarify

How long does it take for us to forget what a conflict was about? We often quickly forget the reason shortly after we come to a resolution. There have even been times when we have stopped in the middle of a conversation because we forgot what we were even arguing about or because we realized we were focusing on two different conflicts.

We need to define the problem because we cannot come to an agreement unless we first agree on what we are trying to agree on. And if our first step is to take it to God to seek His wisdom, we both need to be asking the same question.

In addition, we have to stay focused on one issue at a time. Often during the process, another issue will come forward that has not been resolved, and now we have just significantly complicated the process. Instead, we need to call a time out, identify the second conflict and agree to set it aside for another conversation. We recommend having a notebook beside you to make a note of it.

Also, we need to be aware if an issue that is brought up is one we thought was resolved. In clarifying the issue, we need to figure out if a prior agreement wasn't really an agreement (and why not) or what has changed. If we start off with confusion, it might allow resentment to creep in, which alters the "oneness" mindset we need to begin with.

Is It Mine or Ours?

There is a saying that "if one of you has a conflict, you both do." That is true because of the oneness of our relationship.

Sometimes, though, it is an individual conflict that needs to be resolved one-on-One with God. I (Diane) shared about the irritation I used to feel if Mike was late picking me up. That irritation caused a number of conflicts in our first few years, and we hadn't yet learned how best to resolve conflict. We finally figured out that it was from a childhood wound and that I needed to resolve it through my own healing work, independent of Mike. But I loved that I was able to share my conflict and healing process with him, and that throughout, he was supportive of my work as the healing of my wound brought trust and intimacy to our relationship.

When our actions don't line up with what we know is good and right, there is conflict within ourselves. We can often see that play out in how we interact with others or in the negative emotions we feel toward someone. Our self-intimacy work can reveal to us what we truly believe and where we learned that belief. Our intimacy with God can redirect our thoughts to know and follow His design.

To the extent that our actions have impacted our marriage, we need to work together toward resolution. But oftentimes we can catch it and resolve it before it directly impacts another. When that happens, commit to do the work. If we figure it out quickly, we can create intimacy by sharing the results with our spouse. When the healing is going to take a while, we can create intimacy by being vulnerable while we are doing the work so that they can support, encourage and pray for us. Then when we share the breakthrough, we can celebrate together!

Seek Guidance

When we meet with a couple that is in conflict, our purpose is to teach them how to reach agreement, not to be a referee or make the decision for them. We do remind them that sometimes they will get stuck. If they each hear something different than the other when they seek God's wisdom, they should go back and ask again. But when they realize they're not getting anywhere, they must seek guidance because one or both of them are not hearing God clearly. (Remember, He won't cause separation by giving you two different answers!)

A pastor, counselor or knowledgeable mentor can help bring clarification to the situation—hopefully by leading you through the process and not telling you the answer.

That pastor or counselor also serves a second role—as a witness. When we agree to something, there is always more fortitude to that agreement when it is made in front of someone else. That's why we have witnesses as part of our wedding ceremony. However, the vast majority of our agreements will be made without someone else involved. So, we recommend keeping a journal to record the conflict and agreement. Even writing it down can help solidify the result.

There are two disclaimers regarding the use of a "witness," whether it is a person or a journal. First, it is not that witness's job to hold us accountable; nor should we use that witness to prove something to our spouse. The witness is a source of information for when we discover we are not really, or no longer, in agreement.

The second is to make sure the person we reach out to has our marriage in mind when helping us process. Choose wisely, for the wrong person can cause division through gossip, prejudice or a lack of wisdom. And if we seek individual counsel, our spouse should be aware of and in agreement with what we are sharing and who we are sharing it with.

There is one more thought that is very important with regards to seeking help. Some issues are too big to resolve without expert help. Recently some friends who experienced a major conflict due to infidelity sought out help from highly trained individuals and organizations that have very successful track records. In the process, they have learned that the healing can take 18 months or more to complete. Inexperienced counselors can give us misleading directions or expectations, which keep us from completing the healing or lead us into greater despair.

Of course, a situation that involves abuse, control or a spouse unwilling to take responsibility most often leads to the need for specialized care and counsel. God's design is never for us to be harmed by the person we are supposed to be one with!

Seeking the common goal of intimacy is required. But knowing how and being united in wanting to do it is also imperative to reach and maintain oneness—a properly beautiful marriage.

MAKE IT YOUR OWN

When we first created the Intimate Conflict Resolution process, we ended up with a major conflict. As is often the case, we don't remember today what it was all about. But we do believe that the conflict was effective in creating wisdom for us before we could share the new resolution process with others. It was a good chance to practice what we were about to preach.

It worked, with some minor tweaks. That may have been the only time that we followed the process step by step. It got us going in the right direction, and still today, we try to focus on agreement and intimacy and incorporate the intent of the process we laid out. Even though we created it, we still had to make it our own because of the uniqueness of us individually and of our own marriage.

We also cannot discount the emotion that accompanies conflict. A step-by-step process seems to lack emotion, but it most certainly will be there—before, during and after the issue is resolved. Being aware of it and sharing our feelings (without blaming) can help create an emotional release that may need to happen even before we begin. Taking a breath, or even a short walk, can often keep us from emotionally lashing out at each other.

The more we use an effective conflict resolution process, the more effective we will become in reaching agreement and creating intimacy. Each use is an opportunity to "process the process." When agreement and intimacy have been reached and the emotion of the conflict has dissipated, but how we got there is still somewhat fresh, it is a good idea to be intentional about creating time and space to talk about the effectiveness of the process. Uniqueness of personalities, prior woundedness and the season of life we are in also may impact specific steps that we tried. Learning better communication skills and not operating on assumptions are also effective in connecting well.

As long as we remain focused on our goal of oneness, there are multiple paths to achieve it. Together, we can create a conflict resolution process that leads us toward agreement and to intimacy as a result.

The couples that we recognize as having great joy in their relationship have three things in common: they believe God's design for marriage is the only one that works; they believe their purpose is to love their spouse well, in all circumstances; and they will do whatever it takes to reach agreement and intimacy in all circumstances, including through conflict!

It is no accident that the wisdom shared in this chapter is near the end. It can only be effective when there is intimacy with self, intimacy with God and intimacy with each other!

Our marriage is a priceless gem that is tested and polished by the friction of conflict resolved in a healthy way. We must always remember that the conflict resolution process is most effective when the focus is on what is best for our marriage and with the attitude of loving our spouse to the best of our ability. Then we can both begin to experience the ultimate joy of an epic marriage.

REFLECTION

We strongly suggest you and your spouse both make yourselves familiar with the Intimate Conflict Resolution system in Appendix B. Then talk about the process before you use the process.

- How effective have you been at resolving conflict in the past?
- How does the process we described differ from what you learned growing up and have used in your marriage?
- What will be the most difficult thing to change going forward? Will you do it? Will you give your spouse permission to help you make those changes?

Now for the hard part... Are there any unresolved conflicts festering in your relationship?

- Identify two or three conflicts and then put the system to the test over the next few weeks.
- Don't forget to process the process after each conflict is resolved.
- And don't forget to celebrate when you have reached agreement *and* intimacy!

PART 4

WHAT LIES AHEAD?

CHAPTER 13

EXPECTATIONS AND POSSIBILITIES

ACKNOWLEDGING WHO WE ARE (INTIMACY WITH OUR own self), **determining who we want to be** (*intimacy with God*). **and the results of the three-step change process** (*awareness, conviction, refinement*) **will prepare us to be the complete person it is necessary for us to be so that "***two shall become one.***"**

Northwestern University offers a course simply called Marriage 101. Someone shared with us that the professor would invite guest couples to come in to share with the class, and it always ended with this closing question: "If you could give just one sentence of marital advice to these 200 students before you leave, what would it be?" We thought about what our answer would be to that question and came up with this answer: "It can't be done!"

We can't imagine trying to encapsulate all of our wisdom on marriage in one sentence, or even prioritize one over the others. To write a summary of the last 12 chapters would simply be a repeat of what we have already done.

So now what?

A UNIQUE RECIPE

I (Mike) grew up with an Italian grandmother who made spaghetti that was amazing. When we asked Nonna for her recipe, her standard response in broken English was "you watch." We often did—only to discover that each time she made it, it was different than the time before. What we also discovered is that even though the amounts of each ingredient were never precisely measured, she used the same basic ingredients each time. Many family members tried to duplicate her spaghetti, only to discover that it never tasted quite like Nonna's did. We figured it had to be the unique flavors captured in the cast iron pot that she always used (even though that theory also was proven wrong when others later cooked in her pots).

Diane's spaghetti tastes much different than Nonna's, even though she uses pretty much the same basic ingredients. It, too, is delicious! In fact, the internet is full of spaghetti recipes that use those same ingredients but taste different than both Nonna's and Diane's. They also are delicious—at least to someone.

The internet is also full of quotes on love and marriage, but after spending far too much time searching for that one piece of advice that said it all, we gave up.

Why did God create something so important with this thing called "marriage" without providing a precise recipe that, if followed, would lead to wedded bliss? He did share the ingredients that are required, but He did not include the specific amounts or order. As we look around at other marriages that we admire as well as ponder our own, we have been reminded that marriage is a journey, not a destination. Each couple that enters into marriage embarks on a journey that is uniquely their own.

We are all experiencing a marriage journey that is, and always will be, unique. Still, in order for it to be properly beautiful, it must contain three basic ingredients:

A Bride – The bride is fully committed to becoming more and more intimate with herself, moving toward who she was created to be, and striving to bring herself fully into a covenant marriage relationship.

A Groom – The groom is fully committed to becoming more and more intimate with himself, moving toward who he was created to be, and striving to bring himself fully into a covenant marriage relationship.

God – God is the One who created us and is constantly offering the awesome joy obtainable through the living out of His design and purpose for our marriage relationship.

The amount from the first two ingredients will vary, depending upon how much of ourselves we choose to add to the relationship. That amount will be constantly changing as each of us becomes more and more who God created us to be.

It is the third ingredient that binds all the ingredients together, enhances the flavor and makes the dish a masterpiece. And the more of God we add, the more delicious it will be!

THE ~~END~~ BEGINNING

All of this brings us to the completion of *More Than Great*.

There are hundreds of marriage workshops and programs available to guide couples toward a better relationship, each a unique journey and delicious in its own way. We hope each couple who took the time to read this book feels that the time was well spent and will continue to use the wisdom and resources presented—realizing it is not really the end, but just a new beginning.

So we won't even try to offer one final piece of wisdom that will capture all that has been shared throughout this book. Instead, we want to offer a closing prayer that professes our hope for every marriage journey.

Our favorite Broadway production is *Les Misérables*, which is based on Victor Hugo's book. We leave behind a few tears of joy each time we have seen the musical—especially as we hear the powerful lyrics of the song in the Finale of the musical production, with the show building toward its climax, and we hear these simple, but profound lyrics: "To love another person is to see the face of God!"[1]

And that's our prayer for you...

May you see the face of God in each other as you journey toward a marriage that is *more than great*!

REFLECTION

"Let no corrupting talk come out of your mouths, but only such as is good for building up, as fits the occasion, that it may give grace to those who hear." (Ephesians 4:29)

Write your spouse a love letter.

Share with your spouse your desire and commitment to move together toward epic marriage.

Tell your spouse all of the special qualities you appreciate in him or her, as well as the little idiosyncrasies that make your relationship special.

Tell your partner that he or she is, and always will be, the most special person in your life.

Tell him or her that you will do whatever it takes to create a level of intimacy with yourself, with God and with him or her.

And then *read* the letter to your spouse, so that your encouraging words can give grace to him or her and to your marriage!

Enjoy your epic marriage!

APPENDIX A
THE SPIRIT OF BITTERNESS

A large part of our identity is the result of experiences beyond our control. We are wounded by others; we make a vow as a result of that wound; and then we adopt a behavior based upon that vow. Often, we choose to allow a spirit of *bitterness* to impact our feelings and behavior toward ourselves and others.

Yet, while the experiences may be beyond our control, in essence we've chosen to alter our identity in an attempt to soothe our wound—and often in a way that is harmful to us or limits our growth. More than anything, it impacts our relationships by reducing our level of intimacy.

The work that we do in our relationships can only be fully effective if we address this spirit of bitterness, which may require a deeper understanding of what it is and where it comes from.

We're taught that God is good and that Satan is evil. All of us can envision the image of a person with an angel sitting on one shoulder and the devil sitting on the other, both whispering into that person's ear. There is this constant battle going on inside that person's head. Actually, that image is not that far from the truth.

What the angel is trying to convince us to do is act with the characteristics of God: love, joy, peace, gentleness, justice, honesty, compassion, etc. On the other side is Satan, who is trying to convince us to act with the characteristics of his nature: rejection, hatred, violence, jealousy, guilt, lying, lust, greed, gossip and so on. And although we may think that the war is going on in our head, the truth is, the war is going on in our soul, which is where our will resides. In other words, it's a war between whether we *choose* good (God) or *choose* evil (Satan).

The last time you lied or gossiped or were jealous of your neighbor, did you stop and think that you were *choosing* Satan? In effect, that's exactly what we do.

The apostle Paul tells us in Ephesians 6:12 that "we do not wrestle against flesh and blood, but against the rulers, against the authorities, against the cosmic powers over this present darkness, against the spiritual forces of evil in the heavenly places." Some versions refer to these as "principalities," which are also called demons. It doesn't matter what we call them; rather, it matters that we understand that our war is not against each other but against Satan. Satan wants us to think it's against each other because that will bring division and open the door for his evil army to sneak in—and the impact will be seen in our relationship with our own self, with God and with each other.

Evil came into this world in the garden when Adam and Eve exercised their free will and allowed Satan and sin to enter in. They went from turning to God to know what was right and wrong to suddenly having good sitting on one shoulder and evil sitting on the other! Adam and Eve's behavior reveals the conflicting character traits of God (good) versus Satan (evil). For the first time, lust of the flesh, lust of the eyes and the pride of life are evident—the root problems that we still fight today.

Adam and Eve chose to be disobedient; they chose to sin. And when we choose to sin, we open the door for Satan's demons to manifest their nature through us.

Every example of demons in scripture is one where the demon(s) were manifesting through a person or animal. There are a limited number of them—they can't be everywhere—so they go where they are sent. Think of Satan's hierarchy like you would an army. The demons are the soldiers who take their orders from a sergeant demon and so on up the line. The general is Satan, sending his troops where he thinks they can do the most damage.

But unlike an army in real life, which can force its way into an area with power and without permission, in order for Satan's nature (his demons) to reside in this world, it must have permission from us. We actually give his nature a "place to live" and a form through which to manifest himself.

Those demons will not leave if they are indeed justified in staying—and it's our continuing sin that justifies their right to refuse to leave.

That's pretty scary when you think about it. When we choose sin, we house demons. When others force sin upon us, we can house demons.

How does the spirit of *bitterness* fit into all of this?

Like the other evil spirits, the spirit of bitterness also entered through Adam and Eve. When Adam realized what they had done, it's a good assumption that he felt bitterness toward Eve for giving him the fruit. And when Adam blamed Eve for his sin, Eve was most likely bitter that her husband had not fulfilled his husbandly duties of protection. They blamed each other and blamed God—and likely were bitter toward each other and probably toward God ("Why did He allow that?"). They waged war against each other instead of waging war against the evil one. Thus, the relationship curse began.

Self-bitterness entered the same way. Adam and Eve hid from God; they were ashamed (a characteristic of Satan). We can all probably think of things that caused us to feel shame, which we possibly still do. We can't forgive ourselves for what we did, and we open the door to the evil spirit of bitterness.

Unforgiveness is the door through which bitterness enters. And if it is not stopped, it escalates from there.

Go back to the army example. In Satan's army, there is what is called a principality. Think of it as the platoon, the umbrella spirit that is the identity of that outfit. Bitterness is a principality, a ruling demon. Answering to it are the other demons that also give it protection and provide its armor.

- *Bitterness* starts with *self-pity*. Self-pity carries a negative connotation, but it is really just the acknowledgement of a wound. It is not harmful unless it leads to other layers of evil.
- Bitterness is supported by *unforgiveness* (which opens the door).
- Unforgiveness leads to *resentment*, which is a feeling of ill will toward someone who has harmed us ("I don't like Judy because of what she did" as opposed to "I don't like what Judy did").

135

- Then we decide we need to get even: this is *retaliation*. "I need revenge for the hurt that was caused me." (Again, it is directed toward the person rather than the evil that caused the hurt.) We give our spouse the silent treatment, we exchange harsh words, we don't share a hug when we leave in the morning, etc.
- After that it gets really nasty because retaliation gives birth to *anger*, which gives the evil spirit a voice—an outward indication that reminds the person who was the vehicle of harm that we are not going to forgive, that we resent him or her, and that we plan to get even.
- Once the evil spirit has a voice, the demonic can then easily slide into *hatred*, *violence* and *murder*—the physical manifestations of the principality of bitterness.

What started out as the recognition that someone harmed us, if left unattended, can result in violence and murder (which in marriage is called divorce).

IS BITTERNESS IMPACTING YOU AND YOUR MARRIAGE?

Are you carrying any bitterness right now toward yourself or your spouse? Are you angry at your spouse? Are you planning your revenge? If so, you have opened the door to the principality of bitterness, and it is causing great harm to you and those around you.

The purpose of sharing this truth with you is not to scare you (it's not fun to think there is a demon operating in your soul), condemn you or discourage you; rather, the purpose is to give you insight into the enemy so that you can wage effective war against him. (Our battle is not against each other, but against evil!)

You must know the enemy and how he works in order to thwart his attack. Satan will attack through your mind (your thoughts) in one of three ways:

- He accuses God to you. (Satan will say that God doesn't really love you or that God is holding back from you. That's what he did with the fruit.)

- He accuses others to you. (Thoughts like "If my spouse would only understand, we would get along" take refuge in your mind and lead to corruption in your soul.)
- He accuses you to yourself (in the form of guilt, shame or self-hatred: "Nobody loves me, I'll never get it right").

Paul says to "take every thought captive" (2 Corinthians 10:5), which means to identify whose voice you are hearing. If the voice (that is, a thought) is accusing God to you, others to you, or you to you, then you must identify it as the voice of evil and release it.

How do you do that?

At the end of this appendix, there is an exercise that will lead you through this process. Getting rid of bitterness is only possible through the victory that is ours through Jesus Christ. Through the Holy Spirit, you have been given that same power and authority—the power to release the evil spirit that has taken root in you and replace the evil nature from Satan with the glorious nature of God.

Release

To release the spirit of bitterness, you first have to recognize that you are bitter and how far up the ladder you've gone. Are you resentful or are you angry and ready to retaliate? You have to admit that there is a problem and give it an identity so you know what you're facing.

Second, you must repent of all of the layers of the sin of bitterness. To repent means to renounce your agreement with the evil spirit and turn away from it and receive God's forgiveness. You have to take back the permission you have given the spirit of bitterness to have its home in you.

Then you tell it or them to leave. You take power and authority over the spirits by demanding they leave one by one in the name of Jesus. "Retaliation, be gone in the name of Jesus." "Resentment, be gone in the name of Jesus." And so on, until finally you declare the spirit of bitterness completely gone.

That's the release part. You also need to replace what has just left.

Replace

Remember the story Jesus told in Matthew 12:43–45 where the unclean spirit is driven out but then returns to the empty house with seven more wicked friends? We have to make sure our house is filled up after we sweep out the unclean spirit. What did Jesus do on the cross? He exchanged bitterness for compassion. We must do the same.

After you tell the evil spirit to leave, you then invite the Holy Spirit to fill you with God's good nature. Ask Him to fill you with forgiveness (remembering that unforgiveness was the door that let bitterness in) toward that other person and toward yourself.

Ask Him to fill you with compassion toward that other person to replace the anger. (We often know that we have forgiven when we're able to pray for God's blessing and joy upon that person.) Then go to that person and try to regain fellowship (Matthew 18:15–17).

Then walk in freedom!

Before you begin working through the "Bitterness Removal Guide," we have three suggestions for you to consider.

First, if the idea of identifying, releasing and replacing the influence of evil is unfamiliar to you, we strongly suggest you seek spiritual guidance as part of the process.

Second, forgiveness is not as simple as it is often taught to be. There are levels of forgiveness: simple release, forgiving with boundaries or unconditional forgiveness. Your desire should be to reach unconditional forgiveness in your marriage, but that is often dependent upon your spouse's repentance and counsel for both of you. Again, spiritual guidance may be warranted.

Third, eliminating bitterness does not resolve the underlying issue that created the wound in the first place. It only allows you to enter into the conflict with the right mindset to reach agreement and intimacy.

BITTERNESS REMOVAL GUIDE

Your purpose with this exercise is to first identify any areas of bitterness you are carrying toward your spouse; second, release that evil spirit that is causing it; and third, fill your heart with a Godly vision of your spouse and your marriage.

It is critical that you do this exercise prayerfully, so find that quiet place and the quality chunk of time to proceed most effectively. Make sure you have a separate journal or note paper to capture your thoughts.

1. Begin by asking the Holy Spirit to bring you into a connectedness with your heavenly Father. Sit and enjoy the peace of His presence before you begin.
2. When you feel it's time to move forward, pray out loud the following prayer:

   Holy Spirit, I desire freedom from the bondage of any and all bitterness that I have toward _____ (spouse's name). Please reveal to me now any areas in which I hold any bitterness or resentment toward _____.

3. Sit and listen to what the Holy Spirit reveals to you, making notes for later. If you need some guidance, the following list of relational areas can be useful:
   - Communication and conflict resolution
   - Dreams and desires
   - Emotional intimacy
   - Family and friends
   - Finances and careers
   - Household maintenance
   - Lifestyle
   - Parenting
   - Physical intimacy
   - Spiritual life

4. Once you've made your list, you need to determine how far up the ladder of bitterness you have gone. For each item on your list, ask the Holy Spirit if you are carrying any unforgiveness, resentment, retaliation, anger or wrath toward your spouse in that area.
5. Then get rid of it by praying out loud the following prayer for each area on your list:

In the name of Jesus, in the area of _____,
I repent of my feeling of _____ *toward*
_____ *(spouse's name). In the name of*
Jesus, I renounce the evil spirit of _____
that I have opened the door to (starting with the
level you have determined you are at and moving
up the chain—that is, hatred to anger to retaliation
to resentment to unforgiveness to bitterness). *In the*
name of Jesus, I forgive _____ *(spouse's*
name)   for   _____
(whatever he or she did that you are holding on to).
And I leave it at the foot of the cross, desiring to never
pick it up again!

6. After you have completed your list, thank God for His
   mercy and fill yourself with the Spirit of Jesus by asking
   to be filled with the virtues of godliness that block out the
   evil of bitterness (joy, peace, patience, humility, love, faith,
   hope, etc.).
7. Finish by again just sitting in His presence and enjoying His
   peace and love.

INTIMATE CONFLICT RESOLUTION PROCESS

Through our research and personal experience, we have created this "Intimate Conflict Resolution" process as a step-by-step guide that couples can start with and modify over time as they learn what works best for them as they seek agreement and intimacy.

In order for the Intimate Conflict Resolution (ICR) process to be effective in your marriage, you have to understand and commit to the general guidelines of the process as well as the specific instructions for its use. It is intended to be a tool you can use over and over in your marriage, one that becomes more effective with practice. It is also a tool that you can modify and adapt to your circumstances as you grow together in intimacy.

Using step-by-step instructions may at first seem like you are putting together a new cabinet rather than creating intimacy. However, as the steps become more familiar, the rhythm of the process will become second nature and not so sterile.

GENERAL GUIDELINES

It's a stereotype (one that is often true) that men and reading instructions are like oil and water. Men would prefer to look at the picture and figure it out as they go, which often works, assuming the picture is clear and that they are actually looking at the right picture. But it doesn't work when the picture is fuzzy or is of something different than what they are trying to create.

That's also true when it comes to resolving conflict. If you have an unclear or wrong vision in mind, then the outcome will never look like it's supposed to, and the results will be disastrous.

So, what does healthy conflict resolution look like? There are three basic guidelines included as part of the ICR process that are important to grasp before you begin using the tool.

1. **Understand the goal.** Remember that the intent of resolving conflict in a covenant relationship is *intimacy* and *agreement*, not winning! Because living out a covenant relationship requires intimacy with yourself, with God and with your spouse, the goal of the ICR process involves the same requirement. And because intimacy with God is central to the process, know that the result can only be agreement. God desires oneness in your relationship and will speak the same directions to both of you.

2. **Utilize the correct filter.** When we enter into a covenant agreement, our filter is no longer "what is best for me," but rather *"what is best for the marriage."* The best solution for resolving the conflict will be one that enhances your marriage and glorifies the One who created it. Again, God would never lead you down a path that has negative implications for your spouse or your relationship. Nor would you find joy in something that might bring *you* happiness but cause unhappiness for your spouse.

3. **Maintain the proper mindset.** Conflict starts with a feeling, and it is very easy to get off track when your emotions are leading the way. Your thoughts lead you to your feelings based upon past teaching and experience. Therefore, your mind is what guides you in deciding what actions to take as a result of your feelings. A proper mindset will keep you focused on the right goal using the right filter.

Some thoughts and attitudes to maintain during the process are:

- Walk in *humility* and *grace*. Your marriage is more important than your pride.
- Be *transparent* and take responsibility for your actions. Remove the word *but* from your vocabulary.
- *Connect*, don't convince.
- *Listen* to God and each other.
- Learn what your spouse is feeling and *validate* his or her feelings.

- *Unite!* Remember that Satan wants to separate you, but "...a threefold cord is not quickly broken" (Ecclesiastes 4:12).
- Ask for *help* if you get stuck.
- Know that *it is good*. You're opening the door to greater intimacy.

If your goal is to strive for agreement and create greater intimacy, if you are focused on your marriage first, and if you have the proper mindset, *then* you are ready to begin the seven-step process of Intimate Conflict Resolution. The step-by-step instructions that follow will walk you through the process.

STEP-BY-STEP INSTRUCTIONS

1. **Determine there's a problem.** Conflict begins when you have a feeling that is unsettling. It may be anger, fear, frustration or hurt, or you may not know what you are feeling other than "off." You may know specifically what thought or action it is connected to, or you may not. In either case, *it doesn't matter*. If one of you feels like there is something wrong, then there is! And you need to move forward in the process.

2. **Invite God into it.** Before you go any further, God needs to become part of the process in order for you to reach agreement and move to greater intimacy with each other. It is a simple matter of asking Him to lead, to provide wisdom and to keep you focused on the goal.

   Then *keep* Him involved. Make sure you continually stay in tune with God through regular communication—sharing your thoughts and hearing His. As you sit down to begin Step 3, make sure the Holy Spirit is the One providing the answers you are seeking.

3. **Seek awareness.** This is a critical step so make sure the process is done with intention. Find that dedicated time and place of solitude so that you can think and hear God clearly. Then start asking some questions of clarification, making sure you are prepared to write down the answers as they come forth.

Ask the Holy Spirit to reveal to you the answers to questions like the following:

- What am I feeling?
- Why am I feeling that way?
- Is there a wound or trait that is being triggered?
- Is there an underlying root issue that needs to be addressed?
- Is this an issue that is just mine to "fix," or is it a problem that both of us need to work on together?
- What's at stake for me, or for us, if the problem continues?
- Is there anything else I need to know?

Once you think you're at a place of clarity as to what has happened and why and have an idea of what needs to change, ask God if He will release you to move forward. If you have determined that this is a problem you both need to work on together and if you feel a sense of confidence and peace that God has released you to move forward, then it's time to include your spouse. If you're not quite at peace, there might be more God needs to reveal to you. Spend some additional time seeking awareness.

Note that if you determine this is a problem that is just about you, then your process changes slightly:

- Bypass Step 4 for now and move to Step 5 so that you can continue working one-on-one with God to find the solution.
- Once you have it figured out, then share with your spouse what happened, including what you felt and why, what you determined the problem was, what needs to change and your commitment to doing it. Ask for your spouse's support and encouragement in whatever changes you need to make.
- Then move to Step 8.

4. Invite your spouse into it. Through intimacy with yourself and with God, you have determined that there is a problem, that finding the solution needs to involve both of you, and that you have received great awareness on what has happened. Now it's time to move toward intimacy with each other.

Let your spouse know that you've been working through the ICR process and want to invite him or her in. If your spouse is willing to connect, agree on a time and place when the two of you will not be interrupted and can briefly connect face to face. If he or she is unwilling to connect, it is time to reach out for professional counsel.

This is a good place to add the disclaimer that phone calls, texts, emails or the family dinner table are not acceptable ways to communicate as part of the process other than agreeing on logistics.

In addition, if it seems like there is a problem in the way you communicate with each other, make a point to seek out available resources to help you grow in that area.

The main purpose of connecting at this point is to share all of the available information, define the problem and commit to working together toward the solution that is best for your marriage. It is a time to share what you have been feeling and why, what you've discovered as you have sought awareness, and what you believe the problem is that needs to be resolved. It is also important at this point to remind yourselves of the *guidelines* regarding goal, filter and mindset so that you're properly prepared to join together in the process.

Be transparent in your sharing, making sure you're not putting any expectations of blame or change on the other ("I" statements work best in sharing your thoughts). Be aware that your spouse may need a few moments to process what he or she heard and may need some clarification on parts of it. Your intent should be to share everything that you can.

Once all of the information is on the table, begin to converse about what the real issue is, keeping in mind that you are not trying to solve the problem at this point but instead clearly define what the problem is.

You will know that this step is complete when you both can clearly state what the problem is you are trying to resolve. You may want to write it down to help you maintain clarity and agreement moving forward through the process.

Finish this step by both of you committing to strive for intimacy and agreement and setting the time and place when you will reconnect. End with a prayer of asking God to continue leading the two of you toward oneness.

5. Search for the solution. You've reached the most difficult step of the process because it is filled with emotion. Pride, woundedness, anger, bitterness, defensiveness and even self-protection are all tools that Satan will use to throw you off course. You must stay focused on your goal of agreement and maintain intimacy with yourself and with God in order to realize intimacy with each other.

Step 5 includes two parts that may be repeated multiple times: *a)* seeking God's counsel individually and *b)* discussing your findings with each other.

a. Now that the problem has been clearly stated, each of you should seek God's counsel individually. Begin your one-on-One time with Him by asking for a humble and contrite spirit and committing to Him your desire to reach oneness and greater intimacy with your spouse.

   When you feel you are focused on the goal of what is best for your marriage, ask the Holy Spirit to bring truth to you and *listen* for His reply. (If you have just been invited into the process by your spouse, you might begin by considering the questions offered in Step 3.)

   Write down what you hear, taking time to listen for *all* of what He is telling you. What you hear may include:
   - Understanding how your spouse feels, which will hopefully increase your compassion for him or her.
   - Clarity on your own feelings and their origin.
   - Awareness of your actions and what prompted them.
   - What wound(s) you are working from.
   - Your intentions in the situation—if they were selfish or misunderstood.
   - Your perception of your spouse's actions—if they were selfish or misunderstood.
   - What you need to do so that you can reach agreement.

When you believe that God is done speaking, review and reflect on what you heard. Remember that your own emotions often get in the way of your hearing God clearly, and you should be open to that, especially as you process with your spouse.

Finish this part of Step 5 by checking your heart to see if you are carrying any bitterness toward your spouse. If you are, you need to make every effort to eliminate it before you meet with your spouse.

b. You both should be well prepared and properly focused when you come together at your agreed time and place to connect in finding the solution to your problem. If either one of you needs more time or if a scheduling conflict has occurred, reestablish your connect time as soon as possible (making sure the trait of procrastination or avoidance isn't driving the request).

As always, begin your time together in prayer and ask God to bring you to agreement on the problem of _____. Begin by both of you sharing the counsel that you received from God. *Listen* intently to each other as you share, without disagreeing with what your spouse is saying or focusing on how you will respond. Ask questions if you need clarity on what he or she shared. And *validate* the emotions that your spouse has shared!

After you both have shared, acknowledge where you agree and where you disagree. Be encouraging with each other in the work that you've done and grateful that you have reached agreement where you have.

The challenge now is to connect and discuss those areas of disagreement. Remember that God will not counsel you toward disagreement, so acknowledge that one or both of you has not heard Him completely. Be humble and filled with grace as you move forward in your discussion, always remembering the greater goal of agreement and intimacy. If at any point either one of you is feeling that the process is not honoring to each other or to your marriage, take a breath or take a short break. You *will* eventually reach agreement if you allow the Holy Spirit to lead.

As you reach agreement on certain points of the discussion, again acknowledge and be grateful for that. If you get stuck, set that point aside and come back to it later. If either one of you feels that the discussion has gone outside of the problem you had agreed to solve, gently stop the discussion and agree to get back on track. But first make note of the new issue and agree to address that at another time.

When you both believe you are in agreement on the solution to the problem you have defined, move on to Step 6. But if you're not quite there, go back to individually seeking God's counsel on the specific area of disagreement, coming back together to further process anything that is different than what you originally heard.

If nothing changes after multiple attempts to connect, *seek outside counsel*. Often couples will give in, compromise, agree to disagree or give up at this point, none of which are part of God's design for your relationship. Allow an impartial, trained facilitator to help you reach intimacy by guiding you through the process of reaching agreement.

It is usually wise to establish a realistic time guideline before you begin. If you reach your time limit, either agree to keep going for a designated period or agree on when you can connect again. Distractions of weariness or other prior commitments can often cause a breakdown in intimacy, leading to compromise or stubbornness. Again, the more you use the ICR process, the better you will know your limitations.

6. **Agree and commit.** This step will most often be a continuation of your time together in Step 5. The purpose is to clearly define what the solution is, confirm that you are in agreement, and confirm that you are both committed to following through.
   - Determine if you are in agreement by verbally stating the solution and both of you acknowledging you agree. (Note: If you realize you *haven't* reached agreement, go back to Step 5.) If the solution involves a new goal or direction in your relationship, write it down so that you can periodically review it.

- If the solution requires action on the part of one or both of you, establish how you will monitor the progress being made.
- Then, commit to each other your desire and intent to follow through.
- Finally, acknowledge that you have reached agreement.

7. Heal and connect. You would think that once you reach agreement, you would be finished. But remember that the goal is twofold: agreement *and* intimacy. They are distinct and equally important. What you will find is that you can't have intimacy without agreement, but you can reach agreement and still not have intimacy. When the conflict is minor, intimacy often coincides with reaching agreement. But when the conflict is deep and painful, even after reaching agreement, there is a need for healing from the residual impact of the original injury.

The seventh step requires you to again be intimate with yourself by understanding and acknowledging what you're feeling. After you reach agreement and before you end your time together, pause for a moment and determine if you're bitter or emotionally raw from the process or if you are ready to move forward. Then share your feelings with each other.

- Allow yourself and your spouse to feel what you're feeling. Not being ready to move forward doesn't mean that your process failed; it just means that it's not complete.
- Acknowledge each other's wounds. Regardless of how the conflict arose or escalated, focus on how this may have hurt your spouse. Let your spouse know that you're sorry he or she hurts.
- Take responsibility for the hurt your part in the conflict caused.
- Determine if you need some time to reflect and debrief with yourself and with God. Time can bring healing, and one or both of you may need some alone time. However, communicate what you're doing and when you're done.
- If you have any bitterness or unforgiveness left over from the conflict, you may have opened the door to a spirit of bitterness and need to address it head on. (See Appendix A.)

- Recognize any other issues that may have come up during the ICR process. You may have noted them during your time of processing, but in your debrief time you may realize there is something more. You may have to start the process from the beginning with this new issue (at a later agreed upon time).
- Ask God to bring healing for yourself and your spouse, then let Him draw you back together in an even deeper way than before.
- When you're ready, hug, cuddle, enjoy sexual relations—allow the healing power of physical touch bring you to a place of deeper intimacy.

8. Celebrate! If your ICR process is complete, you will have reached agreement and a deeper level of intimacy in your marriage. You also may have very possibly eliminated an obstacle that could have kept you from growing in intimacy in the future. *Celebrate* your victory! Thank God for each other, for His wisdom and for His creation of marriage.

Give Him the glory and then bask in the reward of great joy!

PROCESS YOUR PROCESS

The more you use this guide or another conflict resolution tool, the more effective you will become in reaching agreement and creating intimacy. It is important to make it work best for the two of you. So within a few days after you have effectively completed the process (while it's still fresh in your mind but the emotion is no longer heightened), spend time evaluating and talking about what worked and what didn't—time, place, individual steps, etc. Then agree to make whatever adjustments are needed so that the next time you use it, the process will be smoother, more effective and less sterile.

Here are some additional thoughts:

The ICR process will become easier and more effective the more you use it.

Remember that it is intended to be a guideline and that you have the freedom to refine it to best fit your own relationship—as long as you're in agreement.

If the issue is minor and if you've become very effective in this process, your process may be completed in a manner of minutes.

You will have times when the ICR process will be ineffective. Don't give up striving for agreement on that issue. When you get there, go back and evaluate where it broke down and why, so that you have a better chance of success next time.

ENDNOTES

Chapter 1
1. *Merriam-Webster.com Dictionary*, s.v. "epic," accessed March 31, 2025, https://www.merriam-webster.com/dictionary/epic.

Chapter 2
1. Kris Vallotton and Bill Johnson, *The Supernatural Ways of Royalty: Discovering Your Rights and Privileges of Being a Son or Daughter of God* (Shippensburg, Pennsylvania: Destiny Image Publishers, Inc., 2017), 134.

Chapter 4
1. "Perfect for Each Other," *Good Will Hunting*, directed by Gus Van Sant (Paramount, 1997).

Chapter 6
1. Mary NurrieStearns, "Exploring Pride, Strength, and Humility: An Interview with Thomas Keating," PersonalTransformation.com, accessed April 10, 2025, https://www.personaltransformation. com/thomas_keating.html.
2. John C. Maxwell, *Developing the Leader Within You* (Nashville: Thomas Nelson, 1993), 63-64.

Chapter 9
1. Jeff VanVonderen, *Families Where Grace Is in Place* (Bloomington, Minnesota: Bethany House, 1992, 2010), 21-22.
2. Christy Bieber, *Leading Causes of Divorce: 43% Report Lack of Family Support*, Forbes Advisor, updated October 17, 2024, https://www.forbes.com/advisor/legal/divorce/common-causes-divorce/.
3. Shaunti and Jeff Feldhahn, *For Men Only* (Atlanta: Multnomah Publishers, 2006), 45.

Chapter 11
1. Shaunti Feldhahn, *For Women Only* (Atlanta: Multnomah Publishers, 2006), 135.

2. Barbara Wilson, *The Invisible Bond* (Colorado Springs: Multnomah Books, 2006), 54-57.

Chapter 13
1. Herbert Kretzmer, "Finale," *Les Misérables*, line 31, updated June 10,
2013, https://www.allmusicals.com/lyrics/lesmiserables/finale.htm.

www.ingramcontent.com/pod-product-compliance
Lightning Source LLC
Chambersburg PA
CBHW071401120626

46546CB00002B/772